kiddiwalks in

Norfolk

D0550189

Angela Youngman

COUNTRYSIDE BOOKS
NEWBURY BERKSHIRE

First published 2012
© Angela Youngman 2012

All rights reserved. No reproduction
permitted without the prior permission
of the publisher:

COUNTRYSIDE BOOKS
3 Catherine Road
Newbury, Berkshire

To view our complete range of books,
please visit us at
www.countrysidebooks.co.uk

ISBN 978 1 84674 278 1

Photographs by the author
Cover photograph courtesy of Rod Edwards/Visit Britain/Getty Images
Maps originally drawn by Karis Youngman

Designed by Peter Davies, Nautilus Design
Produced through MRM Associates Ltd., Reading
Printed by Information Press, Oxford

Contents

Contents

PUBLISHER'S NOTE

We hope that you obtain considerable enjoyment from this book; great care has been taken in its preparation. Although at the time of publication all routes followed public rights of way or permitted paths, diversion orders can be made and permissions withdrawn.

We cannot, of course, be held responsible for such diversion orders and any inaccuracies in the text which result from these or any other changes to the routes nor any damage which might result from walkers trespassing on private property. We are anxious though that all details covering the walks are kept up to date and would therefore welcome information from readers which would be relevant to future editions.

The simple sketch maps that accompany the walks in this book are based on notes made by the author whilst checking out the routes on the ground. They are designed to show you how to reach the start, to point out the main features of the overall circuit and they contain a progression of numbers that relate to the paragraphs of the text.

However, for the benefit of a proper map, we do recommend that you purchase the relevant Ordnance Survey sheet covering your walk. The Ordnance Survey maps are widely available, especially through booksellers and local newsagents.

Introduction

Walking in Norfolk offers tremendous variety. The oft-quoted impression of the county – a flat landscape that stretches for miles, interspersed with a few lakes – could not be further from the truth. As this book shows, you can explore sand dunes, find out about quarrying through the ages, enjoy relaxing woodland walks, as well as roaming around gentle rolling hills. Then there are the occasional sharp escarpments where you can feel as though you are almost walking vertically uphill. And the Broads are a unique man-made environment – a place where sky and water meet.

For children of all ages, walking in Norfolk is a positive delight. There is so much to see and so much to do. Landscapes are varied, with everything from lakes to cultivated fields, offering the chance to see tractors working busily or to enjoy the beauty of an apple orchard.

Keeping kids occupied on the walks is easy. There is plenty of natural history to be found – animals, birds, insects, flowers, trees. Then there is the vast collection of heritage and legends that echo across the region. Norfolk has played a major role in England's history. Visiting the Burnhams will tell you why this is called Nelson's county. Or you could explore the tales of the Babes in the Wood, discover why Henry VIII did not dissolve every abbey, find out about the Romans and learn about the introduction of rabbit warrens to England. Taking the children out and about in this fascinating county will provide something for everyone to enjoy.

Each walk includes notes about where to park and where you can find refreshments. Do remember, though, that things can change and places which are free to park at present could become fee paying. Similarly, pubs and cafés can close or change hands so it is worth phoning to check the current status regarding opening times, etc, if you are planning to visit. Otherwise, take a drink and snack with you to eat along the way.

Above all, enjoy yourselves. Happy walking!

Angela Youngman

AREA MAP SHOWING THE LOCATIONS OF THE WALKS

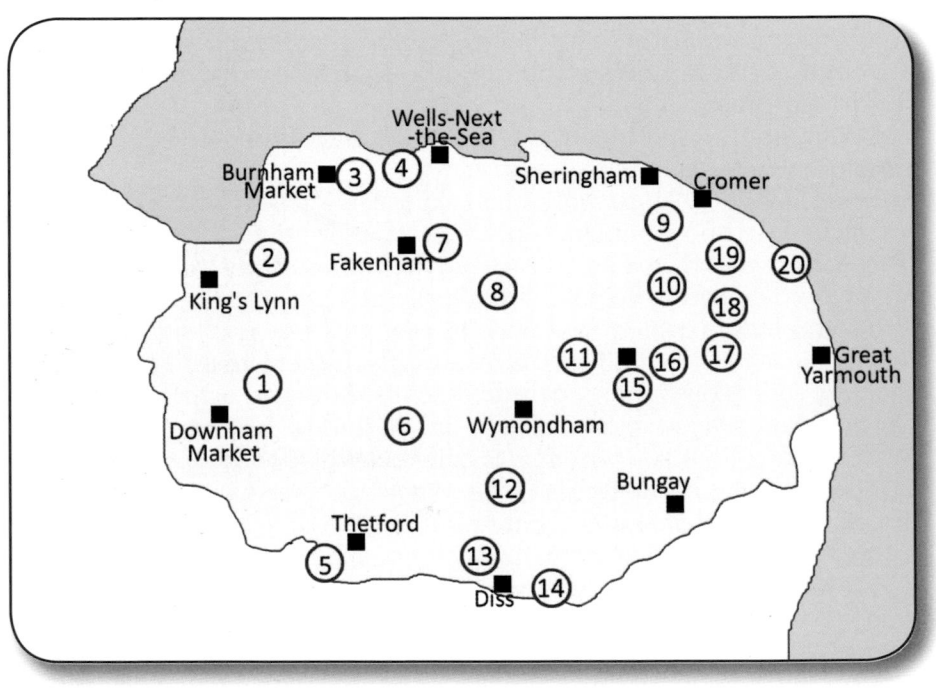

1

Shouldham Warren

A Walk in the Woods

At the start of the walk

Located near to Downham Market, Shouldham Warren occupies a sloping site at the edge of the fens. It marks the transition from fenland to sandy soils and there are some stunning views across the Tall Herb Fen to the River Nar. A good time to visit is in late spring when the rhododendron avenue is in full bloom. The serenity of the woodland can be interrupted from time to time by the sound of fighter jets taking off or returning – RAF Marham is very close by – and the children will enjoy spotting the jets flying high above the trees.

Kiddiwalks in Norfolk

Getting there
Shouldham Warren is situated just off the A134 King's Lynn/Thetford and A1122 Swaffham/Downham Market roads. Follow the signs for Shouldham, continue through the village and head north. A few minutes' drive leads you to the entrance to Shouldham Warren.

Start/Parking The free car park at the entrance to the warren (GR TF 679103).
Map OS Explorer 236 King's Lynn, Downham Market & Swaffham.
Refreshments There are none on the route but in Shouldham village there is the Kings Arms which has a garden and a children's menu, ☎ 01366 347604, and also the Jolly Brewers, ☎ 01366 348134.

Length of walk 2 miles.
Time 1¼ hours
Terrain Firm, sandy and grassy paths, with a slight gradient; pushchair-friendly. Insect repellent is useful when walking beside the Drain.

The Walk

❶ From the car park, follow the track into the warren, and take the first turning to your left, marked by a yellow and red post. This leads down a pathway through a conifer plantation, with

◆ Fun Things to See and Do ◆

Look for **pine cones** and see if you can see any evidence of squirrels nibbling on the cones.

What **animal tracks** can you find? Why not try tracking an animal's footprints and see how far they go along your route?

As you go down the hill towards the car park at the end of the walk, watch the ground carefully. All kinds of **unusual materials** can be found in the rubble that has been used to make up the pathway – tiles, pottery, bits of plastic and large bricks. How many different materials can you find?

rhododendron bushes on the right-hand side. Keep walking straight ahead through an area of silver birch and beech trees until you reach a T-junction.

2 Turn to your right and follow the path through the woodland. Look out for steep mounds in the woods to your right – these contain historic rabbit warrens.

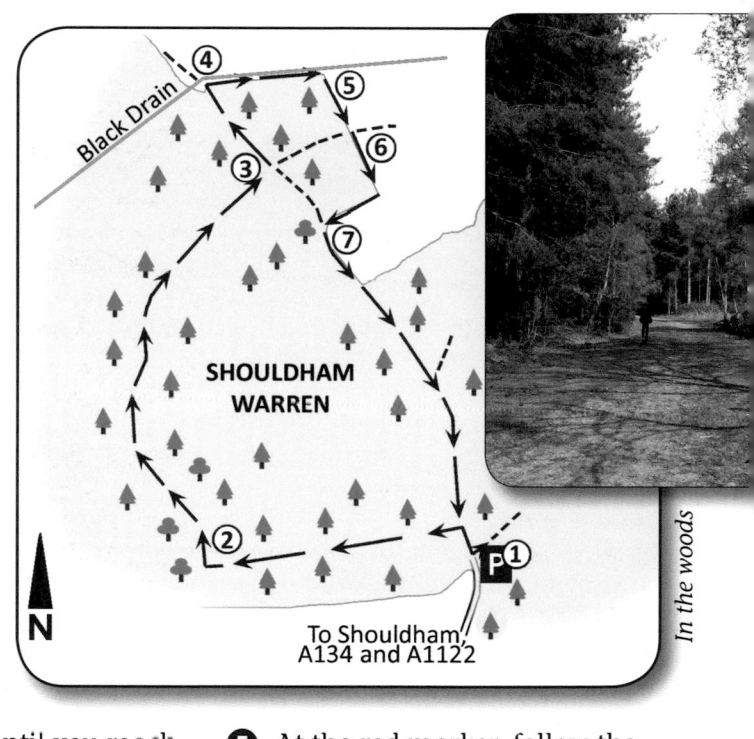

In the woods

3 Keep walking until you reach another T-junction, with conifer woodland straight ahead and a new plantation on your left. Turn left and walk on.

4 At the top of the path you will see a sign marked 'Forestry Commission'. Ahead is a small bridge over the Black Drain. Do not cross the bridge but instead turn right and follow the grassy trackway alongside the drain, keeping the drain on your left and woodland on your right. The drain is quite deep.

5 At the red marker, follow the sandy path to the right between a line of birch trees and up the heather-lined hill towards a stand of conifers. If you find you have gone past a line of mature trees on the left-hand side of the drain, you have missed the turning.

6 At the next crossroads, go straight ahead along the wide pathway.

7 When you reach the next T-junction, turn left. A yellow and red marker can be seen a little

9 ◆

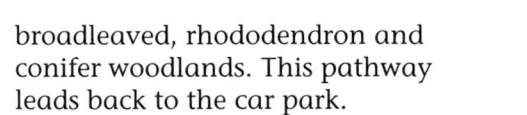

way ahead. The path leads gently downhill, through a clearing and passes through mixed broadleaved, rhododendron and conifer woodlands. This pathway leads back to the car park.

◆ Background Notes ◆

Shouldham Warren is known to have been in existence by 1616. Rabbits were encouraged to live in the area and were protected by warreners who farmed them for their meat and fur. Nowadays, rabbits still live in the warren and play a major role in conserving the local habitat.

There is plenty of **wildlife** to be found at Shouldham Warren, including cuckoos, warblers, deer, grass snakes, herons and lots of wild flowers.

The **Black Drain** forms part of a network of purpose-built drains created over several centuries to drain the fens. For many centuries, the fens were full of marshes and were frequently covered by tidal waters. It was easier to travel by water than by foot as travellers could easily be led astray from safe paths. During the 17th and 18th centuries, a series of drainage programmes in the area were undertaken by landowners. One of the biggest schemes was set up by the Duke of Bedford who hired Dutchman Cornelius Vermuyden to build a sluice at Denver to limit the tidal flow into the Great Ouse River. Marshland soon became rich farmland. The environmental changes did not make everyone happy though – there were many people who had made their living on the marshes. As a result, they opposed the changes violently – the Fen Tigers even blew up the Denver sluice. Their opposition was ultimately unsuccessful. Each time the sluice was destroyed, it was immediately rebuilt. The drains and sluices to be found across the fens are extremely important. If they did not exist, the land would quickly return to marshland.

East of the car park can be seen **huge earthworks and ruined buildings**. These date back to the Second World War and are believed to be the remnants of a temporary camp.

Wolferton Woods and Dersingham Bog

On a Royal Estate

Heading for Dersingham Bog

Walking through Wolferton Woods and the adjacent Dersingham Bog offers definite surprises. The sudden appearance of deep gorges and bogs is totally unexpected as is the vast range of walking surfaces – from bark paths to sandy tracks and steep steps. There is no opportunity for boredom because you never know what the next turn of the path will reveal. A close-up look at the rare plants of the bog can be enjoyed by taking a short diversion onto the special circular boardwalk. Then there is the wildlife – if you are lucky, you may see goshawks or red kites flying high in the sky; or hear the sound of woodlarks. There may be deer, squirrels or rabbits scurrying out of view.

Kiddiwalks in Norfolk

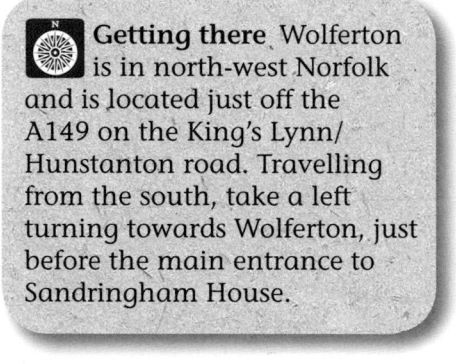

Getting there Wolferton is in north-west Norfolk and is located just off the A149 on the King's Lynn/ Hunstanton road. Travelling from the south, take a left turning towards Wolferton, just before the main entrance to Sandringham House.

Springtime in the woods

Length of walk 2 miles.
Time 1½ hours.
Terrain Mostly firm, but some sandy areas. There are quite a number of steps and slopes, some quite steep; those with pushchairs should use the Wolferton car park.
Start/Parking Scissors free car park (GR TF 668280). If it is full, there is another free parking area further down the road known as Wolferton car park (GR TF 665285).
Map OS Explorer 250 Norfolk Coast West.
Refreshments None on the route itself so why not pack a picnic or head for the visitor centre at nearby Sandringham.

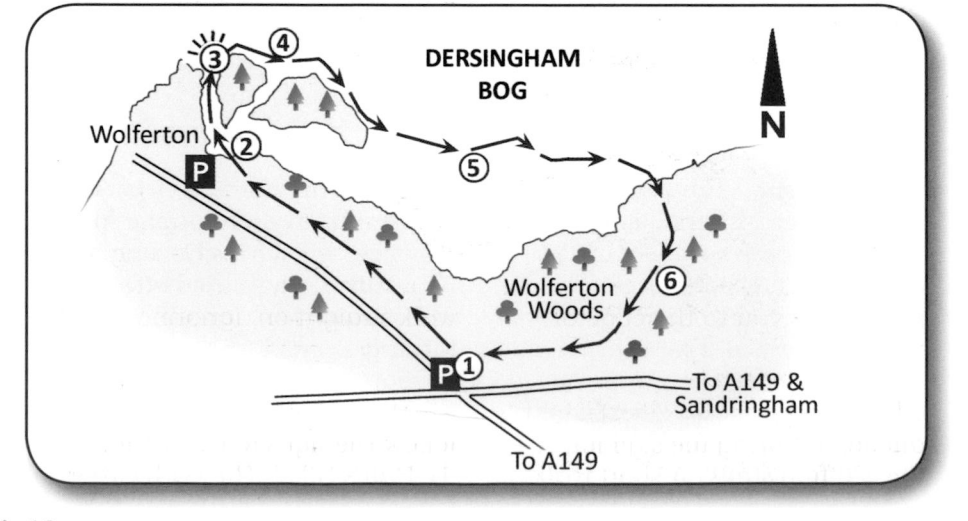

Wolferton Woods and Dersingham Bog

◆ Fun Things to See and Do ◆

Take the circular boardwalk path onto the fragile parts of the bog to see it at close quarters, with a chance to spot many of the more unusual plants growing there. Don't leave the path – the ground will be very, very muddy and you will damage the eco-system.

Make a journey stick as a reminder of your visit. All you need is a stick and some string or wool. You can either tie on different colours and shades of wool at different places on the walk reflecting the colours you see, or you can tie on a small item such as a leaf which symbolises that section of the walk.

At the end of the walk, try retelling the visit from what you can see on your journey stick.

The Walk

1 There is a pathway at the back of the car park, which leads down to the start of the walk. Follow the fenced edge path through the gate. Turn left at the sign marked 'Heathland ramble'. This takes you up some gentle woodland steps. At the top, follow the path straight ahead through the mainly deciduous woodland. The rhododendrons look beautiful in springtime. This winding path leads you to the edge of Wolferton car park.

2 At the signpost walk straight ahead, following the sign for the 'Clifftop stroll'. A short walk through the woods leads to a fence marking the clifftop viewpoint.

3 The views across the gorge are superb – and very unexpected. Leaving the viewpoint, follow the path to the right along the route of the fence. This leads to equally stunning views across Dersingham Bog.

4 When the path diverges, take the left-hand gently sloping path downwards towards Dersingham Bog. Turn right at the bottom and walk straight on, ignoring all other turnings.

5 When the path diverges again, follow the signs to the left marked 'Le Hair's Hike'. The path curves

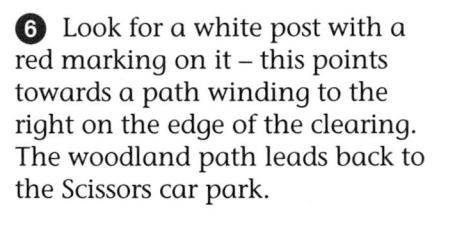

round, following the edge of some sandy cliffs, before beginning to slowly go uphill through very sandy soil, covered with heather. The path leads between two cliffs heading towards a forest of silver birch trees. Keep following the path straight ahead.

6 Look for a white post with a red marking on it – this points towards a path winding to the right on the edge of the clearing. The woodland path leads back to the Scissors car park.

◆ Background Notes ◆

Dersingham Bog is a National Nature Reserve containing a mix of mire (boggy marsh), heath and woodland. It forms part of what was once a vast heathland on an escarpment stretching from King's Lynn to Heacham. The mire, much of which is waterlogged for the majority of the year, is bordered on one side by a steep escarpment. Nowadays one of the largest areas of lowland heath left in Britain, Dersingham Bog offers ideal conditions for a wide variety of plants, birds and animals to thrive – such as the insectivorous sundew, cranberry, nightjar, woodjar and black darter dragonflies. During March and April you are likely to see lots of birdlife, particularly raptors. Sparrowhawks are common, as are buzzards and marsh harriers. Sometimes red kites, goshawks, rough legged buzzards, ospreys and peregrines may be seen. Other bird species to be found in the area include woodlarks, crossbills, bramblings and siskins. Deer, rabbits and pheasants abound.

Wolferton Woods are close to the village of Wolferton, which used to be the location for the Royal Family's railway station before it closed in the 1960s. Each August, the village houses a spectacular Scarecrow Festival.

Just across the A149 is the **Sandringham Estate**, which is owned by the Queen and is frequently used by members of the Royal Family. There are permitted walks across parts of the estate, and it is possible to visit the house and gardens.

3

Burnham Thorpe

Nelson's Land

The old barn at point 3 of the walk

Agriculture combines with naval history to make this a memorable walk. Burnham Thorpe is best known for its connection with Admiral Lord Horatio Nelson, who was born in the village – and the walk leads past the site of his childhood home. As you stroll the byways and quiet lanes of this area, it is easy to imagine Nelson roaming the fields and playing by the stream. It has seen little change over the past two centuries. Agriculture is the major industry round here, and the sight of ploughed fields and crops growing dominate the landscape. Quiet and remote, it seems a long way from major towns and the sea. Yet only a few miles northwards brings you to the coast that Nelson would have known only too well for it was here that he first learned how to sail a ship.

Kiddiwalks in Norfolk

3

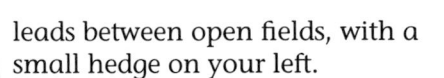

Getting there Take the A149 coast road and turn off southwards to Burnham Market on the B1355, then follow the signs for the nearby village of Burnham Thorpe.

Length of walk 3½ miles.
Time Approximately 3 hours.
Terrain Moderate gradient, rough field tracks and country lanes; pushchair-friendly.
Start/Parking All Saints' church at Burnham Thorpe (GR TF 852418).
Map OS Explorer 251 Norfolk Coast Central.
Refreshments The Lord Nelson pub in Burnham Thorpe offers a children's menu, a large garden and play area, ☎ 01328 738241.

The Walk

1 From the church, turn left and follow the lane to the corner. Look for a stony track on your right-hand side. This is a long farm track, which is like an arrow going straight ahead. It is very stony so take great care not to trip. The trackway leads between open fields, with a small hedge on your left.

2 When you reach the road, cross over and carry on walking along the path. It is very exposed, so can get fairly windy. This part of the walk lasts about one mile and there are very good views across the countryside.

3 Turn right when you come to an old barn. The path is quite wide and leads up and then down a hill. Look for the remains of another old stone building on your left-hand side.

4 When you come to the sign marked 'restricted byway', walk straight ahead between tall hedges. This is much more sheltered than the early part of the walk.

5 At the end of the trackway, turn left and follow the country

The sign marking Admiral Nelson's birthplace

◆ Fun Things to See and Do ◆

Make some little boats out of leaves and twigs and sail them on the stream in the village. Pretend you are Nelson in charge of the fleet.

Which way does the current flow? Is it going up or down? **Carry out an experiment floating some leaves** and identify its direction.

road for a short distance, passing a small pond in the field on your right.

6 Go over a small bridge and turn right, following the signs for Burnham Thorpe. As you walk along the lane, look out on your left for the sign marking Nelson's birthplace. Then carry on walking for about ½ mile until you reach the village.

7 Turn right just after the 30 mph sign, then walk on until you reach a T-junction with a stream in front. Turn left and walk on past the Admiral Nelson pub and the village shop.

8 Take the next right turning. This will lead you back to the church car park.

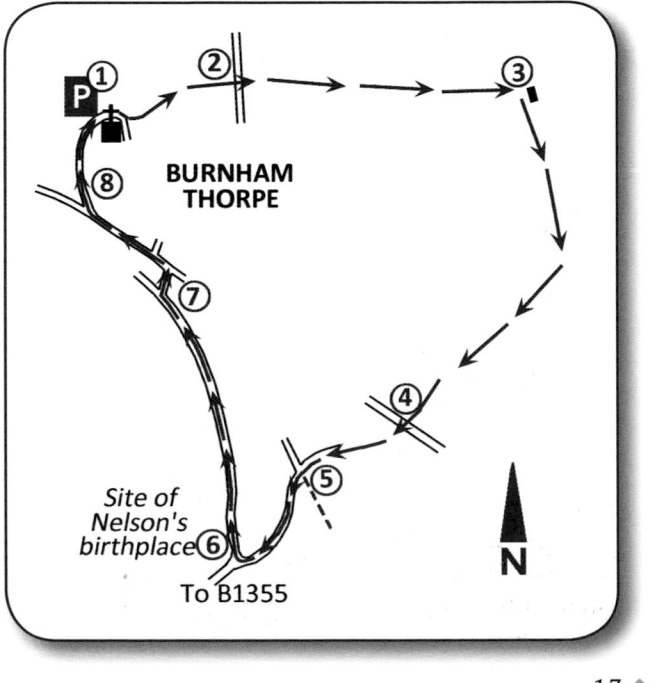

BURNHAM THORPE

Site of Nelson's birthplace ⑥

To B1355

N

◆ Background Notes ◆

Admiral Lord Nelson was born in Burnham Thorpe in 1758. He was the son of the local priest and spent much of his time playing in the fields around the Burnhams. Nelson learned to row and sail a small boat in the creeks. In 1767 his mother died, leaving behind eleven children. Her brother, a naval captain by the name of Captain Maurice Suckling, offered to take charge of one of the children, and Horatio Nelson was chosen. When he was just 12 years old, Nelson joined the Royal Navy. Within a few years, he had risen to the rank of lieutenant. By 1786 he was back in Burnham Thorpe living with his father. With no naval jobs available, he was living on half pay, but when war broke out with France he was recalled to the navy. He was an extremely successful commander, and quickly became an admiral. In 1798, he won the Battle of the Nile off the coast of Egypt and was given the title Baron Nelson of the Nile and Burnham Thorpe. Three years later, he became a viscount after winning a sea battle near Copenhagen. In 1805 came his most famous battle – the Battle of Trafalgar. It was a dramatic and decisive naval engagement: 27 English ships fought 33 French ships, and during the fierce fighting 12,000 prisoners were taken and 20 ships captured or sunk. Nelson was killed during the battle and his body brought back to England. He was given a state funeral and buried in St Paul's Cathedral, London.

Nelson's father was rector of **All Saints' church**. Reflecting its links with Nelson, the church has the right to fly the white pre-1801 naval ensign flag from the tower. The church is worth a closer look. It dates back to the 13th century and has a lovely brass image commemorating William Calthorpe, who died in 1420. There are two small dogs at his feet and two hawks above his head. The church was restored in the 19th century in honour of Nelson. Flags flown by the battleship HMS *Indomitable* at the Battle of Jutland are displayed in the chancel; and the crest of the Second World War battleship HMS *Nelson* is on the wall.

Holkham Hall

A Monumental Walk

Deer on the Holkham estate

Parkland, cultivated fields, woodland, lakes and history – this walk has everything you could possibly want. It is a very peaceful circuit along relatively flat ground. Surprisingly, it is not very well known. Although the hall does attract large numbers of tourists, most people do not venture out into the parkland around it. There are lots of opportunities to stop and relax for a while en route, enjoying the different sights and sounds. The lake is full of ducks and swans, while the adjacent parkland is occupied by eye-catching herds of deer. The obelisks, too, are guaranteed to capture children's imagination. They stand tall and proud within the landscape, yet filled with detailed engravings and sculptures just asking for a closer look. And if you have time and energy left at the end, why not go down to the beach!

Getting there Holkham Hall is located 2 miles west of Wells-next-the-Sea, close to the A149 King's Lynn/ Cromer coast road.

Length of walk 4 miles.
Time About 2 hours.
Terrain Mix of farm tracks, dirt paths, concrete paths, woodland paths; suitable for pushchairs.
Start/Parking The free village car park before you reach the main gates of the Hall and the cattle grid (GR TF 892438).
Map OS Explorer 251 Norfolk Coast Central.
Refreshments There is the Stables café at the Hall (open from April to October) and the Rose Garden café in the village which is open all year.

The Walk

1 From the car park by the almshouses, go through the pedestrian gate and turn left. Follow the path to the large gate marked with the picture of an

Inspecting the obelisk

ostrich with a horseshoe in its mouth. Go through the gate, closing it carefully behind you.

2 About half a mile along this tree-lined track, you will reach a crossroads. Go straight over following the green markers. The track now leads past an open field on your left-hand side and a metal fence surrounding woodland on your right. Look carefully – you may see redstarts in the hedgerows.

3 When you reach an area where paths cross, you will see signs marked 'no right of way' to the left and straight ahead. Turn right and follow the wide path through two fields, heading towards a copse of trees. This is Broom Covert Wood.

4 Follow the track as it winds to the left, eventually passing Great Barn Wood on your right. A little way further on, you will see a large building known as the Great Barn on your left-hand side. Go past the Great Barn, and follow the track as it curves to the right.

5 The track now widens out to become a concrete surface, leading between open meadows interspersed with groups of trees. Listen out for larks in this area during spring and summer. Keep watch to your right and you will

◆ Fun Things to See and Do ◆

Investigate the obelisk and Coke Monument. How many different scenes can be found? What stories do they tell?

Listen out for skylarks in summer. Their liquid sounds are amazing as you watch the birds hovering high in the sky.

How many badges of a white ostrich with a horseshoe in its mouth can you find?

Children used to go out **collecting grasses** for Viscount Coke. Why not see how many different types you can find on your walk? Look for seed heads and grass stems. Are they different in woodland areas compared to the parkland?

Kiddiwalks in Norfolk

4

have your first glimpse of Holkham Hall in the distance.

6 At the crossroads with the Avenue, turn right and walk towards the great obelisk. Built in 1730, it is 80 feet high and stands at the highest point in the park. It is deliberately sited on an axis with the centre of Holkham Hall. The avenue of trees stretches for over a mile.

7 Follow the path as it winds past the obelisk and then down towards the deer park. In springtime, the grass beside the pathway is very pretty as it

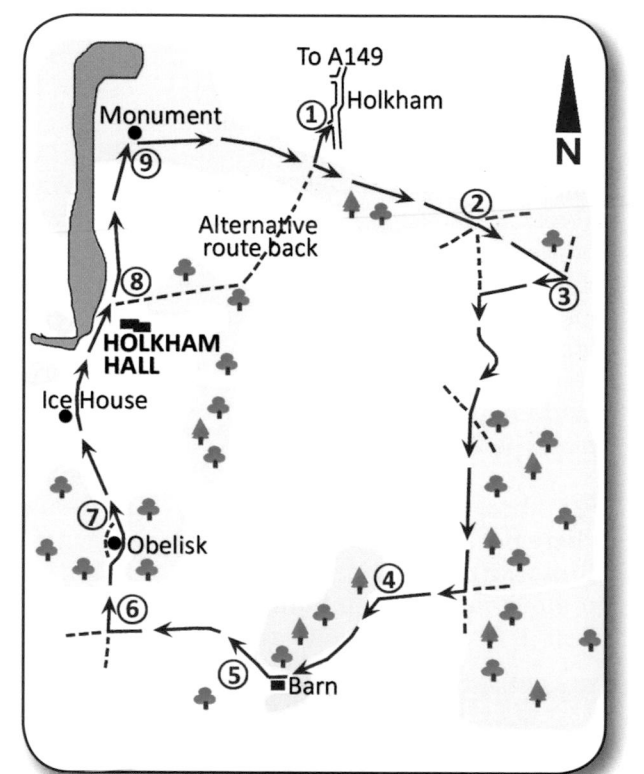

is studded with primroses and cowslips. At the cattle grid, a gate leads through into the parkland surrounding the house. Follow the pathway down towards the lake – and watch out for deer. They can be seen in large herds roaming around the park. Also look out for an unusual thatched building on your left. This is an ice-house. For many years it was used by Holkham Hall to keep food fresh in winter – just like freezers today!

8 When you reach the lake, there are two alternative routes back to the car park. Turning right will lead past the house, toilets and teashop before reaching the main drive, which leads down to the North Gates and the car park. Alternatively, keep the lake on your left-hand side and walk on towards the woodland straight ahead.

9 When you see a path

leading to another obelisk on your left, take that turning and walk straight ahead. It is worth stopping for a few minutes and having a close look at the obelisk. This monument was erected in honour of Coke of Holkham, an 18th-century nobleman who was responsible for many agricultural improvements. It is decorated with statues of animals and carts, and carvings of agricultural scenes. As you walk around the obelisk, turn and face the Hall. This gives a stunning view of the building. Follow the woodland path to the right of the obelisk. This leads past the side of the almshouses and down to the main gates.

◆ Background Notes ◆

Viscount Thomas Coke (later Earl of Leicester) inherited his 300,000 acre Holkham estate in 1776. It was one of the poorest estates in England, with an income of just £2,000 due to the poor soil, which led to a comment 'the thin sandy soil must be ploughed by rabbits yoked to a pocket knife'. Yet this was to dramatically change. Coke was an innovator and keen to explore new ideas. His resultant experiments with agriculture led to a massive increase in income, as well as transforming the role of agriculture in England. He introduced a new four-field rotation system varying the type of crops grown in the fields – wheat, turnips, barley and clover. This vastly improved the fertility of the soil. Apart from rotating the crops and allowing the land to benefit from each type of crop, the turnips were fed to sheep, which compacted the soil and fertilised it with their waste.

Farming is still important at Holkham. The estate has 25 tenanted farms, plus over 1,800 hectares that are farmed directly by the Holkham Farming Company. Agricultural land is generally farmed on a rotation basis involving sugar beet, barley, wheat, beans, peas and potatoes.

The house dates from the 18th century and has been described as the finest Palladian house in Britain. It was designed to impress, with the main façade being 344 feet in length from each of the wings, and possessing a massive six columned portico.

5

Rishbeth Wood, Thetford Forest

Warrens Aplenty!

The straight path through the woods

Rishbeth Wood, Thetford Forest

Rishbeth Wood is one of the many woods that make up Thetford Forest – one of the UK's largest woodland areas – and is managed by the Forestry Commission. It comprises a mix of conifers and deciduous woodland. The conifers are grown very much as a crop and are cut down at regular intervals. The areas that have been subject to felling are immediately replanted with new, young trees, which are left to grow to maturity. The woodland does not comprise one massive forest, instead it is broken up into smaller areas, often linked by a group of trees or heathland. Walking in the forest offers the opportunity to see a variety of environments. This route involves a mix of history and pleasant woodland and heathland settings. It is a gentle, relaxing walk with plenty of opportunities to see all kinds of wildlife.

Getting there Take the B1107 Thetford/ Brandon road. The car park is situated near the golf course. If travelling southwards from Brandon, it is the next turning on the right after High Lodge Forest Centre; while if approaching from Thetford, it is immediately on the left after the golf course.

Length of walk 1½ miles.
Time About 1hour.
Terrain Firm, level walking on natural woodland paths; suitable for pushchairs.
Start/Parking The free car park at Rishbeth Wood (GR TL 840840).
Map OS Explorer 229 Thetford Forest in The Brecks.
Refreshments There are lots of places in the wood to enjoy a picnic.

The Walk

1 From the car park, follow the sandy path alongside the wire netting separating the forest from the golf course. The path soon begins to veer to the right away from the fence. Keep walking straight ahead until you reach the Warren Lodge clearing.

2 Take the left-hand path leading into the forest. Turn left at the pink marker by the bollards. Follow the path, which leads through two different types of woodland – coniferous woodland on your left and deciduous woodland on your right.

3 When you reach the next pink marker, turn right onto a wide

5

Warren Lodge

grassy walkway (or ride as it is known). Follow the path straight ahead between areas of mixed woodland.

4 At the crossroads highlighted by a pink marker post, turn right and walk on until you reach the path leading back to Warren Lodge.

5 Turn right and as you reach the clearing, turn left and follow the path veering right round through the trees and down towards the car park. This gives a lovely view of the lodge set against a tree-lined backdrop. It also offers the opportunity to enjoy walking through a different environment of gorse, heather and cherry trees.

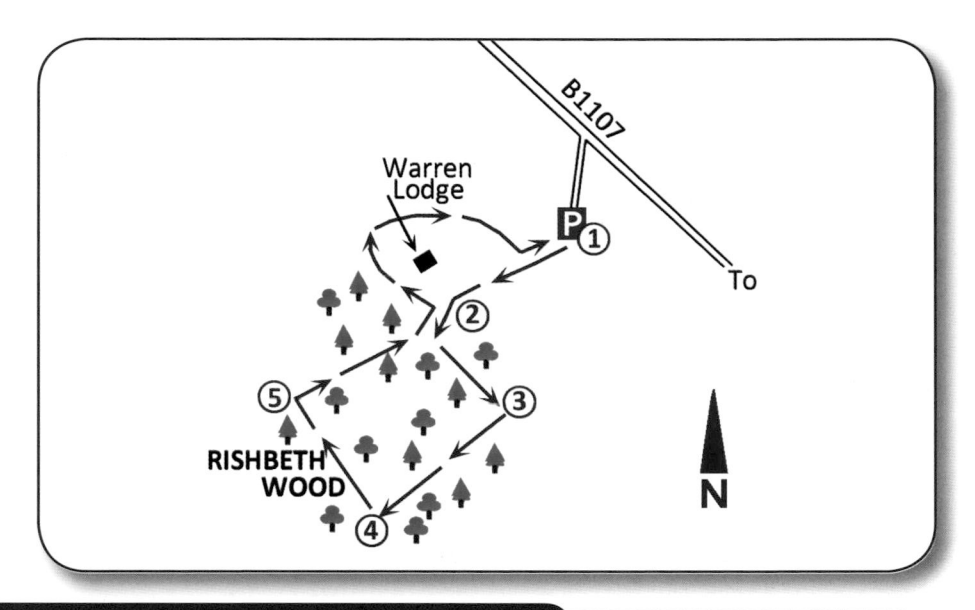

◆ Fun Things to See and Do ◆

Look out for **unusual birds** – stone curlews and hobbys nest in this area.

Between May and September is a good time to see **butterflies** such as the brown and white speckled wood. Other wildlife to be seen in the area includes **deer and rabbits** – many of the latter are the descendants of the original rabbits cared for the warrener employed by Thetford Priory.

Try balancing like a tightrope walker on the tree trunks at the entrance to the forest, near the Warren Lodge clearing.

Make an eco-picture in the sand about your walk. Decorate it with stones, twigs and leaves found around you. When complete, take a photo and leave the picture for others to see. It will eventually decay and return to the natural environment.

◆ Background Notes ◆

The **heathland** seen at the end of the wood was once extensive throughout this area. Until the late 18th century, the majority of the region was heath – open treeless spaces covered with heather, lichens and bracken, which grow naturally on the acidic soils. This heathland is now a threatened landscape and is carefully maintained.

The arrival of the **Forestry Commission** in the region dates back to the end of the First World War. Vast quantities of woodland nationwide had been cut down to provide wartime supplies and there was a need to replace the forests. By the late 1930s the Forestry Commission owned 23,000 hectares of land within the Breckland region. These were ploughed and planted by hand with fast-growing Scots and Corsican pine. There is now an increasing move towards creating native deciduous woodland. Both types of woodland can be seen in **Rishbeth Wood**, reflecting the importance now placed on conservation and recreation. The woodland comprises a mix of pine, oak, beech and larch trees. It is home to numerous animals and birds including muntjac, roe deer, red deer, hares, rabbits, game birds, woodlarks, nightjars, goshawk, siskin and crossbills. Stone curlew breed at the edges of the forest and in the winter, great grey shrike can often be found in the area.

Warreners were very important people in medieval times. They were responsible for maintaining stocks of rabbits for food. Large warrens containing vast numbers of rabbits were set up by the lords of the manor solely for their use. The Breckland area in which Thetford Forest is located contained the largest concentration of warrens in Britain. Warren Lodge in Thetford Forest dates back to 1400 and is made of flint, stone, bricks and tiles. It was built by the Prior of Thetford to provide a home for his warrener so that he could watch over the warren on a daily basis. The warrener would be responsible for making sure that the rabbits were well fed and, when required, trapping them and delivering them to the priory kitchens.

6

Wayland Wood

Babes in the Wood

On the edge of the woods

A n ancient wood linked to a dark tale – Wayland Wood is definitely steeped in history and legend. You can really feel this link with the past as you walk through the trees. This is undisturbed woodland that has seen little change since medieval times. It has links with Vikings and, even more well known, Wayland is where the *Babes in the Wood* story began. It is said that if you listen carefully, you may hear the sound of children crying in the woods. Ghosts are said to haunt it. On autumn days, or misty mornings, the wood is extremely atmospheric and it is easy to believe this is possible. At other times of the year, there are big drifts of flowers among the trees and strange shapes can be seen in the coppiced stumps. Please note that dogs are not allowed in the wood.

Kiddiwalks in Norfolk

Getting there Wayland Wood is located 1 mile south of Watton on the A1075 Watton/Thetford road. The wood and car park are marked by a brown tourist sign.

Length of walk 2 miles.
Time About 1½ hours.
Terrain Flat woodland paths, suitable for pushchairs.
Start/Parking The free car park at Wayland Wood (GR TL 924996).
Maps OS Explorer 237 Norwich or 229 Thetford Forest in The Brecks.
Refreshments
There are none on the walk but the 17th-century Olde Windmill Inn at Great Cressingham 4 miles to the west of Watton has an extensive menu and children's play area. ☎ 01760 756232.

The Walk

❶ Leaving the car park, follow the path into the wood as it winds between the trees.

❷ When you reach the crossroads at the clearing, you need to take the left-hand turning. Listen out for woodpeckers. As you walk you can just about see fields through the trees on the left-hand side. The path winds slightly to the right. There is lots of birdsong, and it is very peaceful.

❸ When the path divides, walk straight on, keeping to the left. Watch out for tree stumps and tree roots on either side. The shapes and sizes are ideal for imaginative ideas about who lives in them! At the bench

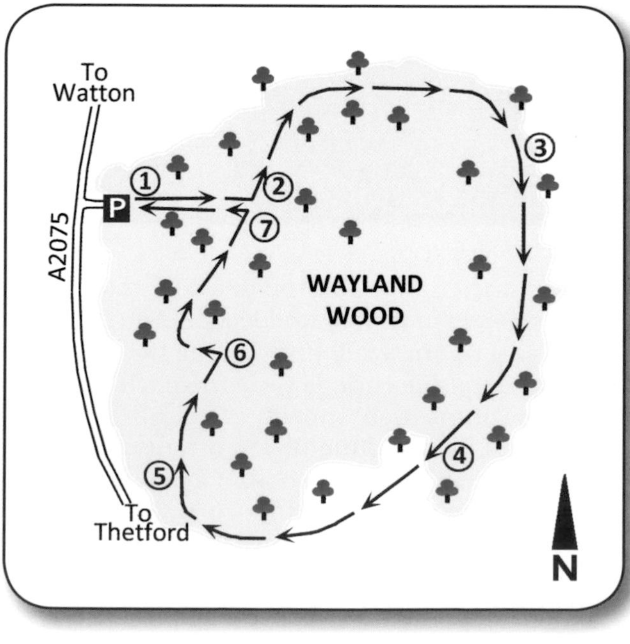

To Watton

A2075

P ①

②
⑦

WAYLAND WOOD

⑥

⑤

To Thetford

③

④

N

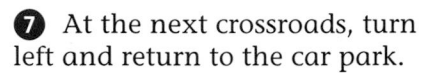

follow the main path, which winds slightly to the left and then goes straight ahead. Look for celandine, wild mint and wild strawberries growing in the verges in season.

4 At the next crossroads, turn right, following the wider path. A white waymarker points southwards.

5 The path winds round the wood, and runs adjacent to the main road. You can hear cars passing, but rarely see them. Eventually the path winds to the right, slowly moving away from the road edge.

6 When you reach a seat, turn left and follow the pathway down a wide grassy path.

7 At the next crossroads, turn left and return to the car park.

A delightful woodland path on the route

◆ Fun Things to See and Do ◆

Look for **unusual-shaped stumps and roots of trees** and places where woods have been coppiced. Many of the exposed roots make arched homes and mini caves – who might live in them?

Woodlands might seem to be mainly green and brown but there is a **vast difference in shades**. Choose a colour. Take a piece of card and some double-edged sellotape with you and put on it a small example of each shade of, say, green that you can find. At the end of the walk, count up and see how many different shades you have found.

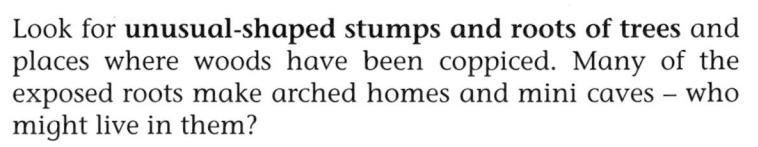

◆ Background Notes ◆

Owned by the Norfolk Wildlife Trust, **Wayland Wood** is a conservation and wildlife area. It is one of the largest woods in south Norfolk and its known history goes back to the Domesday Book. Oak, ash, birch, hazel and hornbeam grow here, together with lots of wild flowers such as bluebells, the yellow archangel, wood anemone, early purple orchid and the yellow star of Bethlehem. The bird cherry trees are a mass of colour in springtime. Wildlife includes woodcocks, lesser spotted woodpeckers, golden pheasants and nuthatches. The wood is regularly coppiced.

Wayland Wood is believed to be the site of the **'Babes in the Wood' legend**. The real story is much darker than the pantomime version. A young boy and his sister were given into the care of their uncle by their dying parents. When they came of age, they would inherit £800, a massive sum in Tudor times, and the uncle decided to rob the children of their inheritance. Two men were hired to take the children into Wayland Wood and murder them. When they reached a clearing, one of the men had second thoughts and tried to persuade his colleague to let the children live. When arguments failed, he killed the other man. Promising to return with some food and to take them to safety, he left the children in the wood, but did not return. The bodies of the children were eventually found huddled together as they tried to keep warm. Legend says that they had been covered with leaves by friendly robins. The story was first published in 1595 by Thomas Millington and is believed to be based on the De Grey family who lived at Griston Hall near Wayland Wood. Two children – Thomas and his sister – had been left in the care of their uncle when their father died, and he stood to inherit the house and land if they died. Four years later, both children died in mysterious circumstances and it was suggested – but never proved – that their uncle had killed them. It is said that at dusk in Wayland Wood, people can hear children calling for help. Who knows what the truth may be – but it makes for a fascinating story.

Fakenham

A Riverside Amble

The three-arched railway bridge at point 4 of the walk

The gently rippling waters of the River Wensum on the outskirts of Fakenham provide a pleasant backdrop to this walk. It is a route that will delight everyone as there is always so much to see and do. The river is edged with fields and woods where a variety of wildlife may be glimpsed. The fields on the far bank of the river are often occupied by farm animals. And for a special treat at the end of the walk – why not visit the Kinnerton chocolate factory shop!

Kiddiwalks in Norfolk

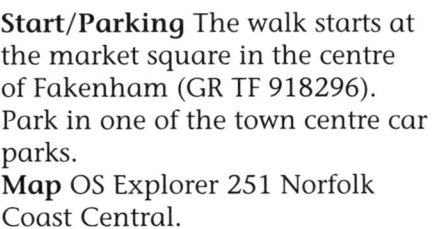

Getting there Fakenham is 10 miles from the north Norfolk coast and can be reached on the A1067 Norwich/Fakenham road or the A1065 Swaffham/ Fakenham road; or from the A148 Holt/King's Lynn road, which bypasses the town.

Length of walk 3 miles.
Time 2 hours.
Terrain Riverside footpaths, narrow in places, and town streets. As some sections can be a bit rough, muddy and slippery, particularly in wintertime, pushchairs might struggle in places.

Start/Parking The walk starts at the market square in the centre of Fakenham (GR TF 918296). Park in one of the town centre car parks.
Map OS Explorer 251 Norfolk Coast Central.
Refreshments There is plenty of choice in Fakenham.

The Walk

1 Leave the market place by Tunn Street and follow the road to the left, which leads down to the old Fakenham mill. This is an 18th-century watermill that bridged the river and was used to grind corn until 1979. It has now been converted to make

◆ Fun Things to See and Do ◆

As you walk along the river, look for **the remains of a concrete bridge**. This was a railway bridge used by the Midland and Great Northern Joint Railway. Many people used to call this railway, the 'muddle and go nowhere railway'! The route went between Great Yarmouth and Sutton Bridge in Lincolnshire.

On race days, **you may spot horses at Fakenham racecourse** on the far banks of the river.

Watch the river carefully. **Can you see any fish swimming by?** There are quite a lot of fish in the River Wensum – fishermen can often be seen along its banks. Maybe you will pass some fishermen on your walk.

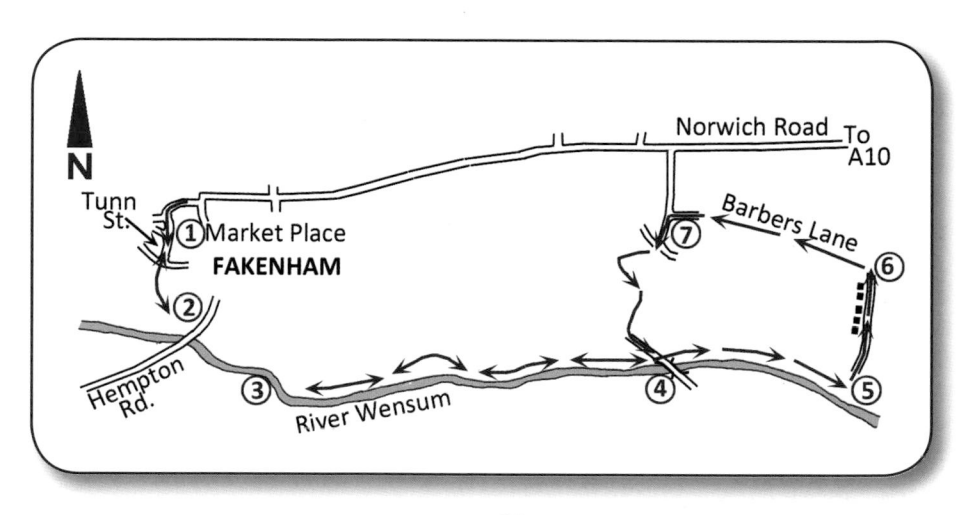

several homes. Keeping the mill on your right, continue walking to Hempton Road.

2 Cross the road and follow the track indicated by the wooden fingerpost behind Fakenham Tyres. This will lead you down to the River Wensum. Follow the track to your right, and go through a recreation area.

3 The river is now on your right-hand side. Go over the concrete bridge, and follow the waymarked grass path along the river. Continue along the river for about a mile.

4 When you reach the three-arched railway bridge, go under the bridge and follow the river path.

5 This path eventually begins to turn to the left away from the river, following a small stream. Cross the stream at the little wooden bridge, and walk up the hill.

6 Follow the unmade road known as Barbers Lane to the left behind the back of a row of houses.

7 At the top of Barbers Lane you will see a signpost. You can now choose from two routes: *either* turn right, then left, for Norwich Road and a walk back into Fakenham by road; *or* turn left and follow the pathway straight ahead. Cross over a small road and you will see the pathway ahead. This leads behind some houses, before reaching open fields. Follow the path through the fields and down

to the river at the three-arched bridge.

8 Turn right and walk back to Fakenham.

◆ Background Notes ◆

Fakenham has been a market town since 1250, and the Thursday market is still situated very close to its original spot around the current market place. Parking on Thursdays can be difficult, as the town is always very busy on that day. There are lots of shops and Georgian buildings. The Kinnerton Chocolate Factory is visible from the start of the river walk – its chocolate shop situated within the Aldiss department store is always popular! The hardest part is choosing between the many varieties of broken and surplus chocolate on offer.

The **River Wensum** is a protected site, classifed by Natural England as a special area of conservation, as well as being a designated Site of Special Scientific Interest. It is a chalk river running within a gently sloping valley. The name is derived from the Old English *wendsum*, meaning 'winding'. This reflects the pattern of the river, as it makes its way gently through the countryside to the south of the town. The area and its linked woodland are home to numerous protected species, including water voles, otters, barn owls, bats and Atlantic crayfish. One of the most unusual creatures to be found in the river is the brook lamprey – a jawless fish.

The **three-arched bridge** was part of the Wymondham to Wells branch of the Great Eastern Railway, which was one of the two railways to serve the town. The route was closed down many years ago and is now disused. Local railway enthusiasts are keen to try to reopen the route as a preserved railway.

Just south of the river is the unusual **Museum of Gas and Local History**. This museum tells the story of manufactured gas, when every town in the country had its own gasworks. Fakenham's works were built in 1846 and provided gas to illuminate the town until late in the 20th century.

Foxley Wood

In and Out the Dusky Bluebells

I wonder! How deep is this muddy puddle?

Foxley Wood is a magical place, perfect for stimulating a child's imagination, as well as offering opportunities to learn about wildlife and the environment. There are lots of tall trees, hidden glades and coppiced areas alive with wildlife, together with plenty of wild flowers such as bluebells and dog's mercury, especially in late spring. This is a very relaxing walk along flat paths, giving a glimpse of what woodlands would have been like in ancient times. In springtime the wood is particularly wonderful. The open paths between trees are covered with carpets of colour, dark blues merging into a misty blue that suddenly becomes vivid as sunlight falls on the bluebells. It makes a dreamy, enchanted setting that everyone will enjoy.

Note: Foxley Wood is closed on Thursdays for maintenance. It is open every other day between 9 am and 5 pm. Dogs are not allowed in the wood.

Kiddiwalks in Norfolk

Getting there Take the A1067 Fakenham/ Norwich road. Follow signs for Foxley village. The wood is a short distance past the village.

Length of walk 2 miles.
Time 1 hour.
Terrain Level woodland and grassy paths; suitable for pushchairs. Welly boots recommended after rain as there may be muddy patches.
Start/Parking The free car park at Foxley Wood (GR TG 049229).
Map OS Explorer 238 Dereham & Aylsham.
Refreshments None on the route so pack a picnic to enjoy.

The Walk

❶ Follow the green arrows from the car park through a coppiced area to the information sign showing maps of the wood.

❷ Turn right and walk straight ahead along a long, wide path, crossing over another wide path and walking through coppiced woodland. This path can be muddy after wet weather.

❸ When you reach a bench dedicated to the memory of Audrey Elizabeth Marchant at the top of the long ride, turn right. The path is narrower and goes through a section of open, deciduous trees. Keep following the footpath as it curves to the left. *For a shorter route*, take the right-hand turning and this will reduce the walk by about ½ mile

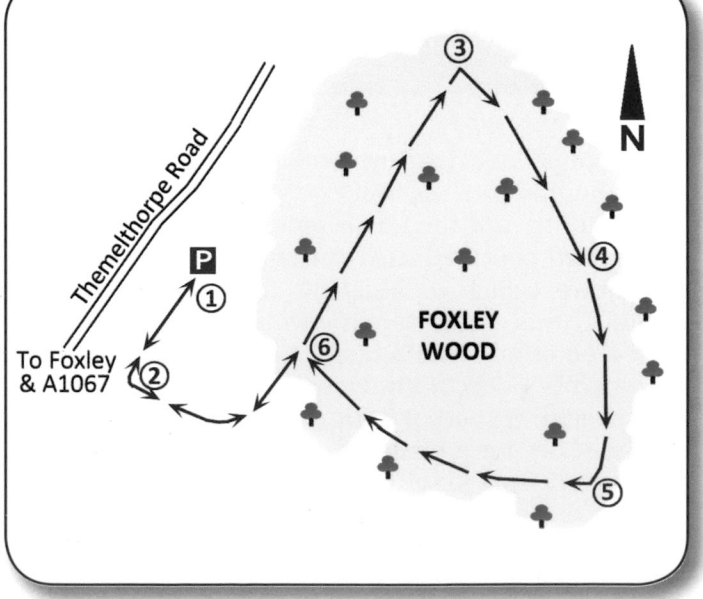

◆ Fun Things to See and Do ◆

Look for trees that have been cut down regularly and now have wide stumps with lots of young, whippy branches. These are trees that have been coppiced. Can you **find the oldest trees** in the wood? These are ancient ash stumps, which are extremely wide.

Why not do a **tree top survey**? Take a pair of binoculars and stand underneath some trees. Use them to look up into the tree tops. It gives a very different view of the woodland.

There are **many different wild flowers** to be found in the wood such as primroses, bluebells and dog's mercury. Look but do not pick them.

and will bring you out into the glade mentioned in point 5.

❹ The winding left-hand path leads over a small bridge across a tiny stream and on through ancient deciduous trees. In springtime, walk slowly and enjoy the sight of the flowers in this area as it is stunning.

❺ When you reach the white marker posts, turn right. The path now goes down a long, wide ride leading into a glade with a path heading to the right. Walk straight ahead. *If you have just arrived from taking the shorter route, take the main path to your right.*

Keep walking straight ahead past the next seat. Look out for a small muddy stream on the left-hand side – ideal for the children to have a little paddle if they are wearing their wellingtons. Beware, though, that it is all too easy to get 'stuck in the mud', which is just what happened to my son. Trying to get out of the mud, his foot actually came out of the boot! The path now winds its way round to the right and will eventually bring you to a crossroads with a 'do not enter' sign for a timber-loading area.

❻ Turn left and walk back to the car park.

◆ Background Notes ◆

Foxley Wood is the largest remaining fragment of ancient woodland to be found in Norfolk. The wood is believed to be over 6,000 years old and many of the trees are the direct descendants of the wild wood that inhabited the site after the last Ice Age. In the Domesday Book it was described as being able to provide 'pannage for 300 swine' and covered an area similar to that occupied by the wood today. It is now in the care of the Norfolk Wildlife Trust and is managed by traditional methods, with regular coppicing. Many of the paths are very wide and are known as rides, designed to give access for removing timber from the wood by horse and cart. The rides divide the wood into field-like sections.

Coppicing means cutting down trees close to the ground to allow new shoots to grow around the edge of the stump. It brings in extra light to the forest floor and encourages the growth of wild flowers. Coppicing is a sustainable ancient practice that creates an endless supply of brushwood. Many of the trees in Foxley Wood have been coppiced for hundreds of years and some of the ash stumps that can be seen are older than the tallest trees in the wood. For over 1,000 years, the woodland has been managed by generations of foresters. Timber from taller and older oak trees provided building materials, while oak bark was used by tanners to turn raw hides into leather. Other trees were coppiced to provide poles, fences and fuel. This management created a perfect habitat for wildlife and flowers because there was always a range of different heights of trees and shrubs.

Over 250 different plant species have been recorded in the wood, including lime trees, field maple, oak, midland hawthorn, dog's mercury, lily of the valley, water avens, primroses, violets, bluebells, herb paris, the wild service tree, meadowsweet, fleabane and purple orchids. The wildlife includes tawny owls, sparrow hawks, green woodpeckers, great spotted woodpeckers, purple hairstreak butterflies, dark bush crickets, blackcaps, warblers, whitethroats and woodcocks, plus the rare white admiral butterfly.

9

Pretty Corner Woods
Ups and Downs

The up and down paths in the wood

Anyone who thinks Norfolk is flat is in for a surprise on this walk – because it involves quite steep gradients! Steep slopes lead down into hollows, and then just as quickly rise up again. Some of the slopes are easily 1 in 4 since the area rises to 315 feet above sea level! You need a lot of energy and strong legs to attempt this walk. But it is definitely worth it, as you feel you are exploring an unknown world. Now and again, when walking uphill, it is worth turning round to enjoy glimpses of the sea in the far distance. This is unusual woodland, which will definitely be attractive to inquisitive and active children. It will also exhaust their energy!

Kiddiwalks in Norfolk

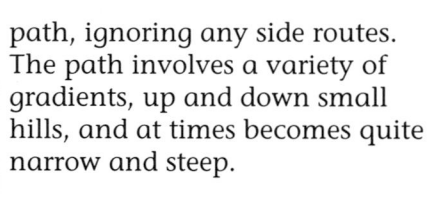

Getting there Pretty Corner is situated on the outskirts of Sheringham on the north Norfolk coast. It is on the A148 Cromer/Holt road. Take the turning marked Sheringham, and then an immediate right turn marked Pretty Corner. Take the first left-hand turning into the car park.

Length of walk 1¼ miles.
Time 1½ hours.
Terrain Grassy paths and woodland ways. Steep gradients both upwards and downwards so not suitable for pushchairs.
Start/Parking The free car park at the woods (GR TG 152413).
Map OS Explorer 252 Norfolk Coast East.
Refreshments There is a picnic area in the car park and refreshments can also be purchased at the nearby Pretty Corner Tea Rooms.

The Walk

1 Leave the car park at the far right-hand side to follow the path into the woodland.

2 Take the path to the right and walk ahead. Keep following this path, ignoring any side routes. The path involves a variety of gradients, up and down small hills, and at times becomes quite narrow and steep.

3 As you come down to the bottom of the steepest hill towards a large number of conifers, you will see a small turning to your right, which is quickly followed by a left turn onto a wider path. This area marks a change from deciduous into conifer woodland. Take the left-hand path, which leads down into a hollow.

4 Stay on the broad track, which winds to the right before joining another track by a wooden bench. Turn left and follow the path round to your right so that you are beginning to go uphill again.

5 Turn right at the next crossroads, so that you are going uphill. This path leads through open woodland, with patches of thicker pine woodland slightly further back. The gradient is very steep but the track is solid and firm. There is a seat usefully placed about halfway up the hill! Turn around and catch a glimpse of the sea in the far distance.

6 At the next junction, turn right. The path now leads

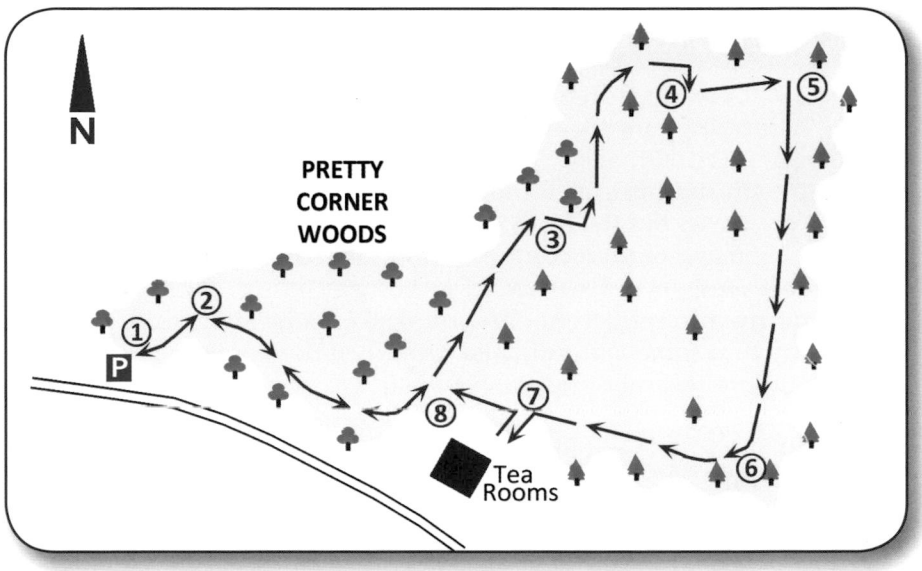

Pretty Wood certainly lives up to its name

◆ Fun Things to See and Do ◆

Look for fallen tree trunks – good for scrambling over and trying to walk along like a tightrope walker!

In autumn, pick **blackberries** as you walk. They may be messy but the fresh, juicy wild fruit have a wonderful taste. Why not fill a container and take some home?

How many different trees can you spot? Look closely and you may find some very unusual ones including pollarded oaks that are several hundred years old.

Pretend you are an explorer as you climb down the steep slopes and into the hollows. What might you see next?

downhill. Continue walking until you see the marker pointing towards the car park or the Pretty Corner Tea Rooms.

7 *If aiming for the tea rooms,* take the left-hand turning, which leads all the way up to them (about five minutes' walk uphill). *If aiming for the car park,* take the right-hand turning and walk straight ahead until the path forks.

8 Take the left-hand turning and this will lead you back to the car park.

◆ Background Notes ◆

Pretty Corner Woods occupy 30.36 acres and are jointly owned by a group of organisations: the Woodland Trust, North Norfolk District Council and Sheringham Town Council. The Woodland Trust is responsible for managing the area, which forms part of the North Norfolk Area of Outstanding Natural Beauty. The woods are unusual in that they are extremely hilly. In places the southern ridge rises to 315 feet above sea level. This is the result of the geological formation of the region. Known as the Holt to Cromer ridge, it is believed to have been formed about 12,000 years ago at the end of the last Ice

Age. With the rise in temperatures, the melted water carried and deposited massive quantities of sand and gravel in the area. Pretty Corner Woods as we know them today first came into being in the early 19th century when they became wood pasture. This meant that the land was grazed, while trees were pollarded regularly for use as timber and firewood. Pollarding is a form of woodland management by which some species of trees can be cut down repeatedly, re-growing into several stems. Some of the resulting oak pollards can still be seen today as you walk around the woods. Since then, natural regeneration and planting have developed the area into extensive woodland.

Nowadays, **the woodland is very mixed**, comprising broadleaf and coniferous trees of varying ages. Some parts are quite ancient, while other areas have been filled with quick-growing conifers. Much of the wood has been poorly managed and is now quite overgrown. Many of the smaller paths are impassable and it is easy to get lost. It is impossible to see the best views that used to exist from the official viewing point as these are now blocked by conifers that have been allowed to get too tall. Underneath the conifers, there is little growing, whereas deciduous areas have underplanting of bracken and brambles. There is also heathland where the sandy soil is ideal for the growth of gorse and heather. A conservation programme is underway to gradually convert much of the site back to broadleaf woodland.

A wide range of plants grow in Pretty Corner Woods including several varieties of orchid, heather, climbing corydalis, oak pollards, grand and Douglas firs, sweet chestnut, birch, goat willow, holm oak, common lime, Norway maple, wild cherry, ash, English elm, sessile oak, Montrose pine, Norway spruce and monkey puzzle. The wide range of trees reflects a history of trees being donated to the North Norfolk District Council and a home being found for them at Pretty Corner Woods. Wildlife is encouraged, resulting in the creation of colonies of long-eared and pipistrelle bats, woodcocks, nuthatches and greater spotted woodpeckers.

10

Blickling
History All Round

We're watching you!

History and nature combine to create a very relaxing walk through a beautiful rolling landscape. Passable in all weathers, the route takes you through ancient woodland, open parkland and by a serpentine lake. There are also the unexpected sights to be found along the way such as a great tower rearing up to your left, and a mausoleum shaped like a pyramid hidden among the trees. Glimpses of the lake are continually teasing – you keep thinking it is closer than it really is. Then once you reach it, you realise that it is bigger than expected because it is impossible to see both ends at the same time. Lots to enjoy along the route – with luck you might even spot birds hanging their wings out to dry!

Getting there Blicking is situated just outside the town of Aylsham in north Norfolk. It is on the B1354 Aylsham to Saxthorpe road.

Length of walk 2½ miles.
Time 1½ hours.
Terrain Firm woodland or grassy paths. Very low gradient. Suitable for pushchairs.
Start/Parking The National Trust car park, free for members, small charge for other users (GR TG 178286). Opening times: Although the parkland is open all year, dawn to dusk, the facilities may be closed during the winter. There is no charge for using the parkland but if you want to enter the house and gardens, entry fees must be paid.

Map OS Explorer 252 Norfolk Coast East.
Refreshments There is a kiosk in the car park which is open during peak periods and the Buckingham Arms pub is close by (☎ 01263 732133). Alternatively why not pack a picnic to eat beside the lake.

The Walk

1 At the back of the main car park, follow the signs to the parkland. Turn left past the houses and go through the white gateway.

2 Follow the concrete track through trees and parkland. Cows may sometimes be seen in the fields. At the Y-junction, take the narrower right-hand path going

◆ Fun Things to See and Do ◆

Look for trees with **unusual bark patterns** in the Old Wood. Bring some wax crayons and paper and take a bark etching. All you need to do is place the paper over the bark and rub down with the crayon. The pattern of the bark will come through onto the paper.

As you pass by the lake, watch carefully in the trees. You may be lucky enough to spot **cormorants drying their wings** after diving for food in the lake – they often sit on high branches with their wings held out. Look too for **dragonflies** in summer.

The mausoleum that can be seen in the woods

towards woodland in the distance.

3 Go through the gate and into the edge of the woodland. Follow the path straight on. This part of the track is very pretty in springtime as there are great swathes of bluebells. Look out for the big tree on your left, which has extremely ornamental bark.

4 Look out for a tower on the left. When you come level with it you will see a seat on your right-hand side, beside a red waymarker. Take the right-hand turning into the woodland. This comprises mainly deciduous trees, and is a very old, ancient wood.

5 When the track next diverges take a short walk to the left to see the great mausoleum, which is about 50 feet high.

This was constructed in 1793 to commemorate the life of the Second Earl of Buckingham. It was built by the Earl's daughter after his death. You can peer through the windows. At the back of the mausoleum look for the memorial stone, topped by a bull, which is the emblem of the Hobart family. After exploring the mausoleum, return to the track and take the track directly opposite, which winds to the right.

6 As you walk out of the wood, you will see a seat on the left-hand side offering good views

over the parkland and towards more woodland ahead. This track leads into a smaller wood known as the Beeches.

7 Continue to walk straight ahead, following the blue arrow. Look for the pile of logs on the right-hand side, which are kept there deliberately for children to lift and see the minibeasts who live underneath. The path eventually leads into a field. Watch out for views of the massive lake. At the far end of the field, you will find a small track on the right-hand side.

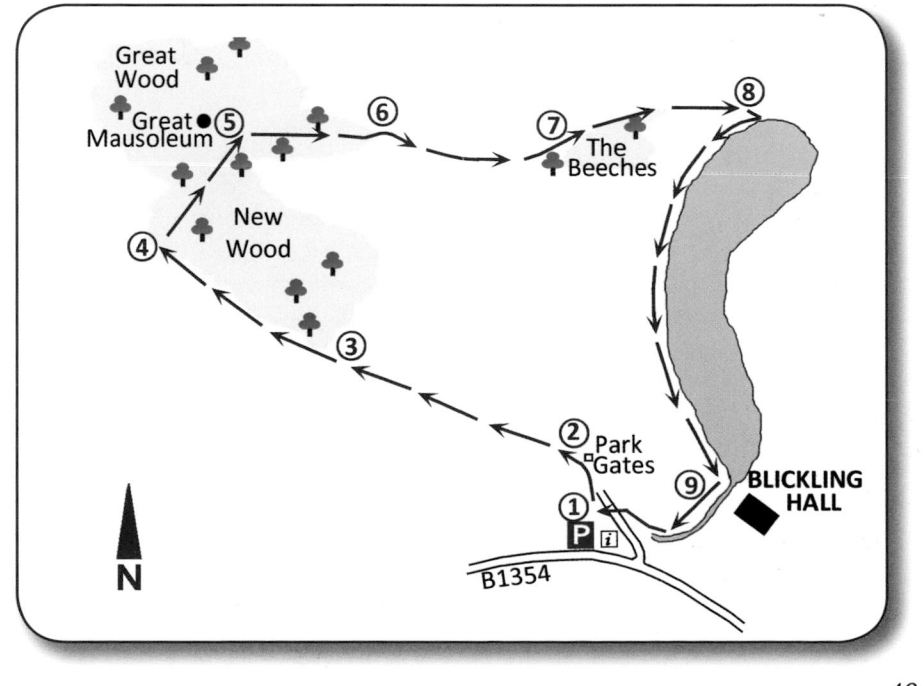

8 Turn right, heading towards the lake. At the lakeside, there are several seats and this is a good place for picnics. Leaving this spot, turn right and go through the gate. Follow the track along a grassy path through a field. Access to the lake with its thick reed beds for nesting birds is prevented at this point by a fence. Go through the next gate and walk straight ahead, keeping the lake on the left. Just before the end of the lake, enjoy the views of Blickling Hall. Then turn right and follow the track away from the lake. This is a firm grassy track, which leads into the parkland.

9 Keeping the house and fence on your left, follow the path straight ahead. Go through the gate at the bottom of the field and turn left, following the line of the wall. Turn right by the thatched house and follow the path back to the car park.

◆ Background Notes ◆

Today **Blickling** is a stunning Jacobean mansion – but it has a much longer history. In the 16th century, it was owned by the Boleyn family and Anne Boleyn herself may have been born here. Anne was Henry VIII's second wife and when she failed to give him a son, Henry's affections turned elsewhere. He wanted to replace her. Knowing he could not afford another divorce, he sought to find other grounds for her removal. Eventually she was put on trial for treason, and executed. Even her own father voted against her. Now each year on the anniversary of her execution, Anne arrives at Blickling Hall in a coach drawn by four headless horses with a headless coachman. The coachman is said to be Anne's father, Sir Thomas Boleyn. Reports have also been made that her ghost has been seen roaming the house and grounds.

The massive **Blickling lake** was specially constructed in 1711 for the Second Earl of Buckingham. It has an unusual serpent-like shape. This was deliberately chosen as it is meant to impress everyone. Whichever end of the lake you stand at, you cannot see the other end; thus creating the impression that it is actually a river.

11

Ringland

Hills and Meadows

Heading for the river

The beauty of the Ringland valley is easily overlooked when driving along the busy A47. Hidden away down narrow roads, as it is, not many people know it exists. You approach along country lanes surrounded by thick woods high up in the Ringland Hills, then dip down into the valley through which a wide river gently flows, surmounted by a picturesque bridge. The narrow roads can be off-putting to many drivers, but it is worth persevering as Ringland offers a wonderful country stroll up and down hills, along country lanes and exploring field tracks, as well as marshland. There is plenty of wild life for the children to spot along the way, including swans and ducks on the water.

Kiddiwalks in Norfolk

A47 Norwich/Swaffham road about 5 miles from Norwich. At the roundabout at the end of the Norwich bypass, take the turning towards Ringland. At the next road junction, turn left and drive straight on until you reach the village and see the Swan pub on the left. These are very narrow roads with passing places available for cars.

Length of walk 2½ miles.
Time Allow 2 hours.
Terrain Varied gradients, stiles, field tracks, grassland and country lanes. Suitable for pushchairs though may need to be lifted over one of the stiles.
Start/Parking The Swan Inn (GR TG 136139). For those not patronising the pub, there is a small car parking area beside the river. **Map** OS Explorer 237 Norwich or 238 Dereham & Aylsham.
Refreshments The

Swan Inn at the start of the walk has a large garden and an extensive menu. ☎ 01603 868214.

The Walk

1 Starting at the Swan, turn left and walk down the road past the village green. On the way, look for the house with the monkeys in the garden! Keep walking until you reach the church of St Peter.

2 Turn right and follow the road past the village hall on the left-hand side. This building used

◆ Fun Things to See and Do ◆

Swans and wild ducks can often be seen feeding beside the river. The shallow stream is very clear and you may see some fish swimming by.

Walking along the road through the village, watch out for **the house with lots of monkeys** in the garden. When we walked by, there were toy monkeys of all sizes hanging from trees, perched on lamp-posts and sitting in doorways and windows.

At the village green, **look at the sign**. It contains the names of many of the people who live in the village.

Depending on the time of the year, there are lots of **wild flowers** to be seen in the fields and near the river. Look for bluebells, wild primroses, cow parsley, Queen Anne's lace, the pink and white flowers of the campion and the bright yellow flowers of the lesser celandine, as well as plenty of hawthorn blossom. You will also see **butterflies** flitting to and fro among the flowers in summer.

The monkey tree!

to be known as the Reading Room and also served as the Methodist chapel.

3 At the end of the row of houses, look for a sign, marked 'The Street'. Beside it there is a wide sandy track going uphill. Take this track; it is quite steep. At the top of Royal Hill, there are stunning views across Ringland to the south and the valley of the River Wensum to the north.

4 As you walk past a house on your left-hand side, look for a grassy path to the right of the hedge. This leads towards a stile marked with a yellow marker.

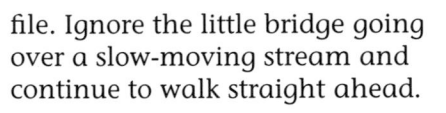

The stile is an unusual one where you have to pull the sides apart and walk through rather than climb over. Turn right and follow the path beside the hedgerow. At the end of the field, go through another stile. The track winds to the left towards a grove of poplar trees. Beyond the poplar trees, the path leads through a low-lying marshy meadow, offering views of the river in the distance. At times the path becomes quite narrow and you have to walk in single file. Ignore the little bridge going over a slow-moving stream and continue to walk straight ahead.

5 When you reach a house with a lamp-post beside it, turn right and walk on.

6 A short way down the track, look for a signpost on the right marked 'Footpath'. Follow this path to the left and it will bring you back into the main street, beside the Swan.

◆ Background Notes ◆

Ringland is an ancient village, mentioned in the Domesday Book. The church of St Peter dates from the 14th century and has some very beautiful stained glass. Its most well-known priest was Parson Woodforde, author of the book, *The Diary of a Country Parson*, which gives an insight into the life of 18th-century Norfolk. He was rector here from 1776 to 1803.

The Ringland Hills and Royal Hill were formed at the end of the last Ice Age from gravel deposited here by the retreating ice. The soil is very sandy, with lots of smooth flint pebbles. Artist Sir Alfred Munnings described the area as 'one of our loveliest districts of all in this pleasant country'. One of his most famous works is entitled *Ponies on Ringland Hills*.

The village grew up around the **river crossing**. Originally this was a wooden footbridge and a ford for horse-drawn traffic. The importance of the valley and its surroundings is reflected in the fact that it played a defensive role during the Second World War. Rare concrete 'tank traps' from the war can still be seen by the banks of the River Wensum.

New Buckenham

A Hidden Castle

Beside the moat

When you are driving down the B1113, New Buckenham is a tempting place to stop and walk. A lovely large common with a children's playground nearby is clearly visible as are the pretty flint houses and ornate market cross. The hidden treasure of the castle comes as a surprise. This is a very relaxing walk through a variety of environments – from quiet village streets to meadows, common, fields and of course around the moated castle. It is a route full of surprises and makes you wonder just what is hidden round the next corner.

Kiddiwalks in Norfolk

Getting there New Buckenham is approximately 15 miles south of Norwich, on the B1113 road.

Length of walk 2½ miles.
Time About 2 hours.
Terrain Mix of paved streets, grass, field edges, and rough common which should be fine for pushchairs except perhaps in winter or after heavy rain. There is a deep moat alongside the route at point 4.
Start/Parking The walk starts from the market place (GR TM 088904) and there is free parking on street in the centre of the village or by the edge of the common.
Map OS Explorer 237 Norwich.
Refreshments There is a choice of pubs and cafés in New Buckenham.

The Walk

1 Turn left by the signpost at the top of the market place, towards the church. Go past the flint-stoned church, and follow the road round the corner of Grange Road, by the Rosemary Lane entrance.

2 Turn left, keeping the church on your left-hand side. This will bring you back into the market place. Walk down to the end of the road and continue down

◆ Fun Things to See and Do ◆

Explore the castle. How would you defend it against invaders?

Can you find the **gargoyles** on the church? These can be seen on the belfry windows and the tower. The gargoyles were used to direct water from the roof onto the ground. When it rained, water would shoot from the gargoyles' mouths.

If you are here in the summer months, can you spot any colourful **dragonflies** flitting across Spittle Mere?

The stream on the edge of the common is an ideal spot for **paddling** when the weather allows.

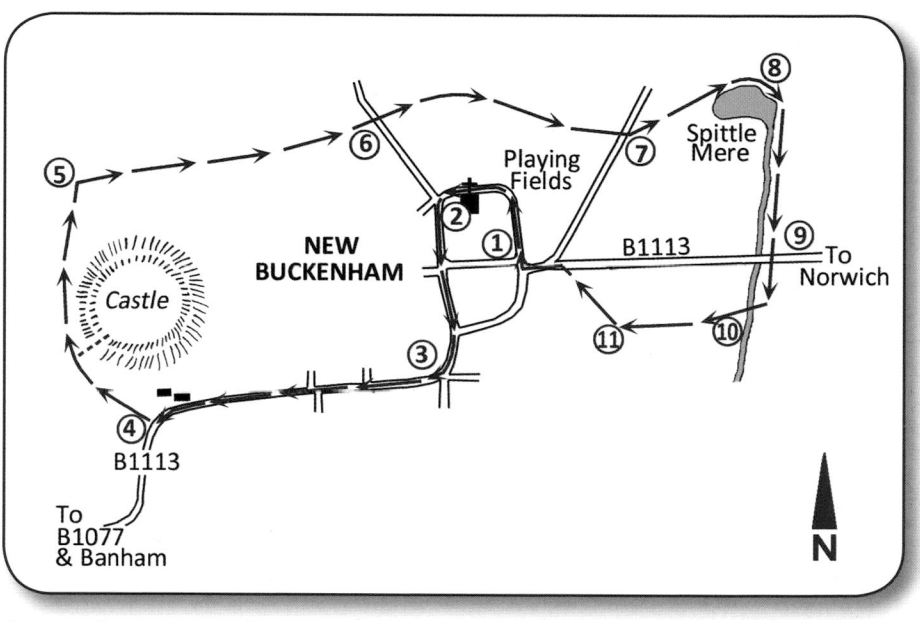

Queen Street, past the King's Head pub.

3 Follow the road round to the right and along King Street. Look for the almshouses on the left-hand side of the road, which have a Dutch gable design on the roof.

4 Just past the garage, you will see a track beside a converted barn. This leads away from the road. Follow the track straight on and watch out for the moat on your right. The area around the moat is now overgrown with trees, but the moat is still full of deep water – so ensure that children take care. The path leads along the edge of the moat and there is a little path to the right, which will eventually lead down to the moat itself.

5 At the top of the field, bear to your left and aim for the houses in the distance. The path crosses over a small ditch. Keep the ditch on your right-hand side and follow the path along the field edge.

6 Cross Cuffer Lane and follow the track up Moat Lane. The track goes round to the right past the village hall. Go straight across the playing field and you will see the gated entrance to the common on the far side.

Walking the greenway

7 Passing through the gate, walk north-eastwards, aiming for Spittle Mere, which can be seen outlined between trees in the distance.

8 There is a small boardwalk around the northern part of Spittle Mere. Follow the path to the top of the bank and turn right. Walk down towards the B1113 on your right, crossing the stream by the ford or footbridge. This is a grassy pathway, which at times is very boggy and makes for rough walking.

9 Go through the gate near the little stream. Cross over the road and go through the gate on the other side. Head towards the stream and keep it on your right-hand side. Aim for the footbridge or ford over the stream.

10 Walk diagonally across the common, aiming for the gate at the far left-hand corner.

11 At the sign for Tas Valley Way, turn right and follow the track back to the road. Turn left and follow the road a short distance down into the centre of the village.

◆ Background Notes ◆

New Buckenham was laid out as a planned settlement with its own market, by William D'Albini in 1145. It has maintained its original size and plan. Most of the streets are still lined with 15th- to 17th-century houses, and some still have overhanging upper storeys.

The **Market House** is a lovely building. It was originally a court or toll house used by the villagers during market days. It was rebuilt around 1700, and has an overhanging first storey balanced on eight Tuscan columns. Evidence of its use as a court can still be seen. In front of the Market House is a whipping post complete with arm clamps.

The **castle** is quite big and is in a traditional motte and bailey style. The keep is believed to be the earliest and largest circular keep in the country. Nowadays, only the lower storey remains but originally it was two storeys high. As you look across the gates, you can see the tall walls rearing up in front. These are about 40 feet high. All the earth used to create the walls of the castle keep was taken from the moat. You can go inside, but you have to ask at the garage for the key to open the gates. There is an admission charge.

New Buckenham Common is one of the largest in Norfolk and was formed in the 12th century to provide grazing land for the new village. It is still lightly grazed by cattle, and is managed by the Norfolk Wildlife Trust. The common forms a flower-rich meadow with many green winged orchids. A prominent feature of the common is the presence of the hollows dug for clay and flint, which have now become ponds. The largest of these is **Spittle Mere**, which is home to crested newts, as well as the many songbirds living in the nearby trees.

The common is bisected by a long straight road, which was laid out in 1779 as a turnpike. One of the **original milestones** can be seen as you cross the road after leaving Spittle Mere.

13

Burston

The School That Went On Strike

Burston Strike School

The longest running strike in history combines with orchards and open fields to create a fascinating walk through the Norfolk countryside. This quiet village just north of Diss was the setting for a 25-year-long strike by school children! The walk begins beside this unusual village school, which is beautifully maintained to give a very green setting. Although it looks as if you are about to drive onto the grass, it is actually growing through reinforced plastic that protects the ground. Cars leave no trace of their presence on the village green. The walk is particularly lovely in springtime, when the orchards surrounding the village are full of stunning white blossom.

(GR TM 136831)
Map OS Explorer 230 Diss & Harleston.

Getting there Burston is just to the north of Diss and is signed westwards off the A140 Diss/Norwich road.

Length of walk 2 miles.
Time About 2 hours.
Terrain Mixed gradients, lots of stiles, field paths and public roads. Some fields may be occupied by grazing animals. Owing to the number of stiles, this walk is not pushchair-friendly.
Start/Parking On the village green beside Burston Strike School

Refreshments Village shops, plus the Burston Crown pub which offers a children's menu, ☎ 01379 741257.

The Walk

❶ Starting on the village green, turn right and walk along the pavement until you reach Market Lane.

❷ Turn left and follow the road between houses. This road turns into a dirt track between fields. In spring, there are lots of primroses to be seen.

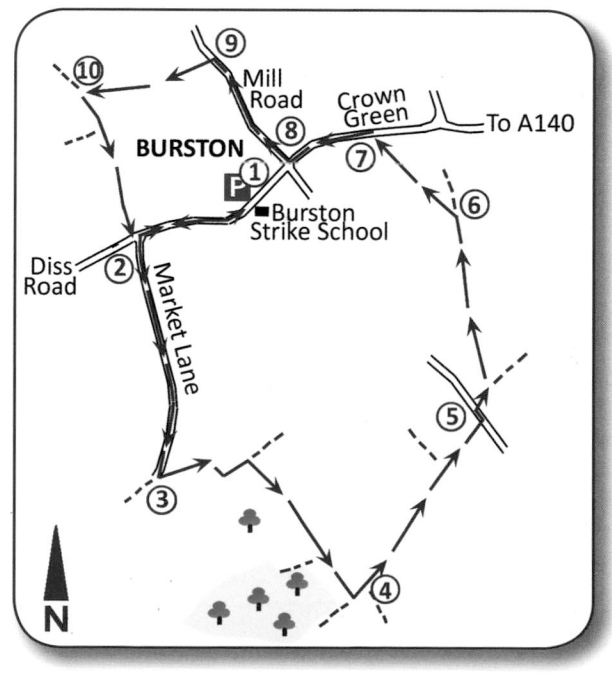

❸ At the public footpath marker, leave the main track, turning left and following the grass path diagonally between two fields. At the next post turn right along the field edge. Cross the plank footbridge over the ditch. Follow the field track along the edge of the field and head for the bridge with a handrail. This crosses over a deep ditch.

4 Turn left and walk up the field towards the houses in the distance. A railway track runs alongside the far side of the field. This is the Norwich/London railway line and express trains use it frequently.

5 Turn left at the road then immediately right onto a public footpath. Look for a footpath sign beside a garden edged with white bollards. Follow the footpath to the right, leading to a stile. Go over the stile, and keeping the hedge on your right-hand side, walk to the far corner of the field. Grazing animals can sometimes be found here. Look for the markers on the fence indicating you need to turn right, then turn immediately left. Walk on, keeping the hedge on your left, the pond on your right. Head for the stile beside the gate in the far corner, which is roughly diagonal to where you entered the field.

6 Once through the gate, turn left across a narrow plank bridge, which leads into a playing field. Walk diagonally across the field, aiming for the car park.

7 At the road, turn left into

◆ Fun Things to See and Do ◆

Look at **the front wall of Burston Strike School**. It contains lots of stones inscribed with the names of people who helped fund the school, including Russian novelist Leo Tolstoy, author of the classic story *War and Peace*.

How many **different types of stile** can you find on the route?

Investigate a hedge. What can you find in it? Take a stretch of hedge and look closely at it. Can you find any nests? How many different types of plant can you find? Are there any wild flowers growing at its base? Is there anything there that should not be there? (Look for rubbish.) What insects are present? Are there any berries? This exercise can be repeated at different points in the walk to see if there are any differences.

Springtime blossom

Crown Green Road and walk on past the school.

8 At the crossroads, turn right into Mill Road. There is a signpost pointing towards Mill Green. Go past Burston chapel and Waveney Animal Feeds.

9 When you reach the end of the houses, look for the stile on your left-hand side. There is a marker for a public footpath. Cross the stile and walk straight ahead. The route takes you between orchards and a vineyard.

The path is quite wide and straight. In spring, the sight of so many trees in blossom is stunning. At the bottom of the path, go through the gate and turn right then left at the waymarker. Walk straight ahead.

10 Go over the next stile to join a track called Green Lane. Turn left and walk straight down the hedge-lined track until you reach the road, where you will need to take a left turn back to the car park.

◆ Background Notes ◆

Burston Village School is the unlikely setting for the longest strike in history, lasting 25 years. The strike began in 1914 when the teachers were dismissed by the school management committee. The teachers – Tom and Kitty Higdon – had complained about poor conditions in the school, particularly inadequate heating, lighting and ventilation. On one occasion the managers accused a teacher of lighting a fire without permission – she had done so to dry the clothes of children who had walked three miles to school in the rain. Of the school's 72 children, 66 went on strike – and never returned to the school. Instead, their original teachers continued to teach them in a variety of locations including a marquee. Burston Strike School was built in 1917 by public subscription including donations from many unions. This allowed the teachers to continue their work. The strike school continued until 1939, when Tom Higdon died. Kitty was unable to continue and the remaining 11 pupils transferred to the council school. An annual rally commemorating the strike is held at the site on the first Sunday in September.

Orchards have been part of the Norfolk landscape since medieval times. The owners of the existing orchards are carrying on an ancient farming practice, growing fruit for eating, cooking, storing and making cider. Orchard trees play an important part in the landscape, providing homes for a wide range of invertebrates, hole nesting and insectivorous birds. The trees also act as hosts for mistletoe and lichens.

Evidence of climatic change can be seen in the presence of the **grapevines**. This is one of the northernmost vineyards found in England, and is able to thrive this far north as a result of the drier summers that are being experienced.

Waveney Animal Feed may not look very large but it is a big business exporting animal feed to the Far East and Iceland.

14

Billingford, near Diss

A Windmill and a Lost Village

Tractors at work

This is a pleasant walk along country lanes and bridleways in south Norfolk. The hedgerows are full of wild flowers such as Queen Anne's lace, cow parsley, ox eye daisies and poppies. The sound of birds is ever present, as the thick hedgerows offer lots of nesting areas. Not to be missed is the opportunity to see Billingford windmill – the last mill in Norfolk to grind corn by wind power. There are memories too of lost villages. Take a short diversion to explore the remains of St Mary's church and think about the community that once stood beside it.

Getting there Billingford is less than 3 miles east of Diss, just off the A143 Diss/ Bungay road.

Length of walk 3¾ miles.
Time About 2 hours.
Terrain Tarmac, concrete and field tracks, small gradients. Although there are no stiles, there are several footbridges and these are quite narrow. The route can get muddy in winter. Not suitable for pushchairs.
Start/Parking The layby beside

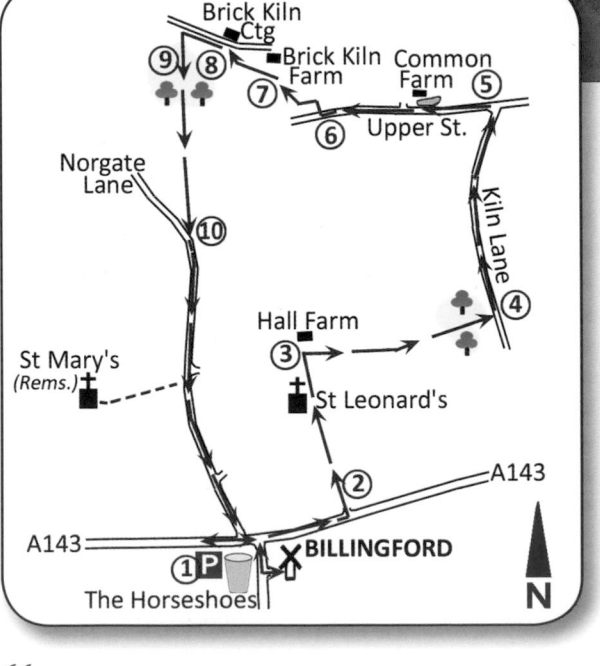

the Horseshoes pub (GR TM 165786).
Map OS Explorer 230 Diss & Harleston.
Refreshments The Horseshoes pub is open all day and has a beer garden, ☎ 01379 740414.

The Walk

1 Turn right out of the layby, then a sharp right again to visit Billingford

St Leonard's, the church without a steeple

windmill. Returning to the footpath beside the main road, follow it to the right to its end. Cross the road. This is very busy, so it is important to take great care.

2 Immediately in front of you is a tarmac track with a signpost indicating a church. Follow the track up the hill, passing St Leonard's church on your left. Keep walking until you reach the end of the track.

3 Billingford Hall Farm can be

seen in front of you. Turn right onto a restricted byway known as the Angles Way. Follow the track between hedges and open fields, passing a copse of hawthorn, sycamore, ash and oak trees on your left. In springtime look for the beautiful horse chestnut trees full of pink flower spikes.

4 At the junction with Kiln Lane, turn left. This is a quiet country lane, passing beside hedge-lined fields.

5 After passing a thatched

◆ Fun Things to See and Do ◆

Visit the windmill. You may be lucky and see its sails move as it grinds corn. Find out how the sails can be adjusted to meet the direction of the wind.

Look for the **various types of pond** along the way. At Common Farm there is a traditional duck pond situated just outside the entrance to the farm. This is quite deep and edged with reeds. A very different type can be seen in the field just beyond Brick Kiln Cottage. This pond is a natural one, edged by trees in the middle of a field.

How many **different kinds of tree** can you find along the route? Hawthorn, horse chestnut, sycamore, ash and oak can all be found, together with a wild rose hedge. The horse chestnut trees are lovely in spring, with pink and white flower candles. There are lots of oak trees along the paths, so why not **hunt for acorns in the autumn**?

house on your left, you will see a road junction with a post box straight ahead. Turn left into Upper Street and walk on past the entrance to Common Farm. Take a minute to stop and enjoy the sight of ducks swimming on the pond.

6 Just before the houses at the corner of the road, turn right at the Norfolk Walks waymarker onto a track alongside a field edge. The track heads towards trees in the distance. There is a small ditch, about 4 feet deep, on the left-hand side. Follow the path straight ahead over two bridges, aiming for the brick building in the distance. Ignore all waymark and footpath signs.

7 Just before you reach Brick Kiln Farm, look for a narrow plank bridge over a ditch on your left-hand side and beside it is a hedge. The bridge is a bit hidden among the undergrowth. There is a handrail. Cross the bridge and walk straight ahead, following the path of the hedge until you see a yellow marker pointing towards the road opposite Brick Kiln Cottage.

8 Turn left at the cottage and walk down the country road for a couple of minutes until you reach a waymarker pointing to a field track on your left.

9 Walk straight ahead down the field track. It will lead past a small pond hidden among the trees, and over a footbridge. This is a straight path with hedges on your right-hand side and an open field on your left. At the end of the path, it turns to the right and leads out onto a narrow country road – Norgate Lane. Listen out for birds in the hedgerows as you pass by. The banks at the sides of the lane are filled with wild flowers.

10 Follow this lane down to the main A143, and you will be facing the layby beside the Horseshoes. Along the lane, look for a footpath pointing to the right. This will lead you to the remains of St Mary's church.

◆ Background Notes ◆

There has been a **windmill** at Billingford for centuries. This one was built in 1860, following a gale that destroyed the earlier post mill. It is a five-storey brick building with four sails. The mill stopped grinding corn commercially in 1956 – the last mill in Norfolk to do so. It has since been restored by the Norfolk Windmills Trust and grinds corn on an occasional basis. ☎ 01362 869394 for details of open days.

St Leonard's church is unusual in that it has no steeple. At first sight, it is easy to mistake it for a house with its rendered flint walls and red tile roof. The surrounding walls are edged with topiary balls. It is a very compact little church set amongst the trees.

The **tower of St Mary's church** marks the location of the **lost village of Thorpe Parva**. This village had been deserted by 1789, a victim of changing agricultural patterns. It is worth the short diversion to explore the ruins of St Mary's, which stand out amid the fields around them.

15

Caistor St Edmund

In Boudicca's Footsteps

On the bank of the River Tas

Just south of Norwich is a hidden town, one that was totally unknown until the mid 20th century when a plane spotted unusual lines in the earth. The quiet fields, edged in the distance by the A140 and the Norwich/London railway line, hide a Roman town. Climbing up the massive ramparts, which are all that is left of the town walls, and looking out across the sheep grazing peacefully beyond, it is fascinating to think that this was once a bustling community with soldiers marching, shops and craftsmen, houses with children playing and even an amphitheatre tucked away in the far corner. Youngsters' imagination can run riot here – what was it like in those days? And then, of course, there is the fun of exploring the banks of the River Tas, seeking out the little rapids. Stimulating yet peaceful, this is a wonderful place for a walk.

Getting there Caistor Roman Town is 3 miles south of Norwich, near the A140. From the A140 turn off beside the Dunston Hotel, follow the road to the end, turn left and then follow the road northwards.

Length of walk 2 miles (and an extension to reach the river to the south of the site is possible).
Time Allow at least 1½ hours.
Terrain Grassy paths. Part of the route involves lots of steps so it is not suitable for pushchairs.
Start/Parking Caistor Roman Town free car park
(GR TG 232033).
Map OS Explorer 237 Norwich.
Refreshments None available on the site but the diversion to the river at point 3 of the walk provides a delightful picnic spot.

The Walk

❶ Take the gateway to the right of the car park leading you directly to the walk around the town walls of Venta Icenorum. There is a steep flight of 37 steps leading to the top of the walls. Once at the top, turn left through the gateway. This brings you onto the wall walk, with quite a big drop down to your left. As you walk along the path the Roman town is on your right. Nowadays the site is grazed by sheep.

❷ Halfway along the wall, there is a stile giving entrance onto the field site. It is located just where the main south gate would have been in the town. There is a useful notice-board giving details about the town. If you cross the stile, you can walk straight across the field to the north gate, or turn west to the west gate. Staying on the main path leads you round the edge of the town site until you reach the west gate and another information notice-board.

❸ A lovely choice awaits you – carry on walking or turn right for a slight diversion down to the River Tas. This is an ideal spot for paddling (although the water is usually very cold!) as well as tree climbing. A seat provides a good spot for picnicking or relaxing while the children play. Watch the water bubbling over the small rapids. Look out for the bat boxes on the big tree. A stile leads into an adjacent field where you can stroll along the river.

When you are ready to resume the wall walk, turn left at the big rock outcrops and be amazed at the size of the building work.

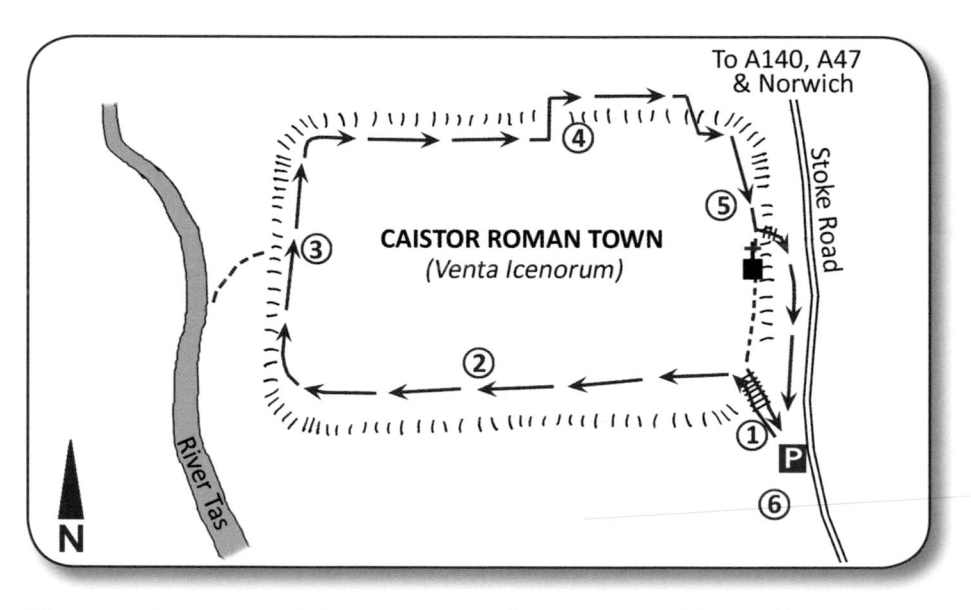

To A140, A47
& Norwich

Stoke Road

④

⑤

CAISTOR ROMAN TOWN
(Venta Icenorum)

③

②

①

P

⑥

River Tas

N

These are just some of the examples of the Roman walls that can be seen as you walk and are some of the most impressive.

The remains of the wall on the northern side of the town reach a height of about 20 feet.

◆ Fun Things to See and Do ◆

Sheep graze the site all year. In the spring, see how many different coloured lambs you can find. We spotted white, black, black and white, and white with black and brown splodges. See how much **sheep's wool** you can find caught on fences or lying on the ground.

Play Pooh sticks in the river and see whose stick passes the rapids first.

By the river there are some **lovely trees perfect for climbing** – although you might get surrounded by a flock of curious sheep!

I'm the king of the castle!

4 As you pass the north gate to the town, the path diverts leftwards to the base of the walls, before leading to another flight of shallower steps to reach the top of the wall. Continue along the top of the wall walk to the entrance to the church.

5 Here you have a choice: *either* you can continue walking straight ahead to the church, which is well worth a visit to see the way in which Roman construction materials have been incorporated into the walls, *or* you can turn left past the war memorial, then sharp right into a wooded walk way leading back to the car park.

6 If you want to continue walking, cross the car park and leave by the gate opposite the main entrance. This will lead you onto a path below the walls and down to the river and the rapids below the west gate. Keeping the river to your right, there is a pleasant stroll along the riverbank and into the next field, which once housed the Roman amphitheatre. Bear diagonally to the left until you reach the gateway. This will bring you into the large field below the car park. You need to walk diagonally across to the far right corner to reach the exit. This field was the location of archaeological excavations in 2009/10.

◆ Background Notes ◆

Venta Icenorum was a major Roman town occupied from the first to the fourth centuries AD.

When the Romans left Britain in the 4th century, the site fell into disuse. The incoming Saxons preferred a site on the banks of the River Wensum, which led directly to the East Coast. This became the foundation of the modern day city of Norwich. Venta slowly returned to grassland and many of its bricks and tiles were later used to build a church on the corner of the site. As years passed, the site was forgotten, indicated only by the Roman word Caistor (or fort) in the neighbouring village name of **Caistor St Edmund**.

The site was rediscovered in the 20th century by aerial photography during a drought in 1929 that revealed the outlines of the town buildings. A small excavation within the town area confirmed this and objects found during the dig can be seen in Norwich Castle museum. Smaller digs took place in 2009 and 2010 identifying more workshops and buildings – and a skeleton – in the fields situated to the left of the main town site.

Boudicca was queen of the Iceni tribe who lived in the Norfolk area. Originally independent of Roman rule, the region was annexed by the Romans following the death of Boudicca's husband. Boudicca and her daughters were abused by the Romans. She retaliated by leading the Iceni and various other tribes in a dramatic revolt against Roman rule, burning Colchester, London and St Albans before meeting the Roman legions in battle. The Romans proved victorious.

Whitlingham Great Broad and Old Wood

A Wildlife Wander

Racing along the river

Walking beside the peaceful waters of Whitlingham Great Broad, it is hard to believe that twenty years ago this was a hive of mining activity as diggers excavated vast mounds of gravel. From Neolithic flint mines to gravel extraction in the 20th century, this is a walk through mining history – and its results. Just behind the Old Wood is the busy A47 bypass, built using gravel from the area now occupied by tranquil water scenes. As soon as the gravel was extracted, the area was restored and made into a stunning country park containing the first new broads to be created since medieval times. Smooth, level surfaces around the broad make way for forest paths that wind up hill and down dale – ideal for tiring out energetic kids. Younger ones will be happy simply walking round the broad and seeing the wildlife.

16

Getting there Turn off the Norwich outer ring road just north of its junction with the A146 and head towards Trowse Newton. Very soon, turn left down Whitlingham Lane to reach the visitor centre on the left, with the car park beyond.

Length of walk 2¼ miles around the Great Broad; the woodland walk adds another ¾ mile.

Time Allow 3 hours for the full walk.

Terrain The broad walk is flat, firm and suitable for pushchairs. The forest section of the walk involves woodland tracks and steep gradients and therefore is not pushchair-friendly.

Start/Parking Great Broad car park (this is located immediately past the visitor centre); a small charge is payable (GR TG 254077).

Map OS Explorer OL40 The Broads.

Refreshments These are available at the visitor centre during the summer months and at other times dependent on the weather and staffing.

The Walk

1 Leaving the Great Broad car park at the bottom, head for the broad, which is straight ahead. Turn left past the visitor centre and follow the path along the broad. On the left you will pass the remains of Trowse Newton Hall, which was visited by Edward III and Queen Philippa of Hainault.

2 Turn right at the next signpost, walking towards the Outdoor Education Centre. You will pass by the Little Broad on your left, keeping the Great Broad on your right.

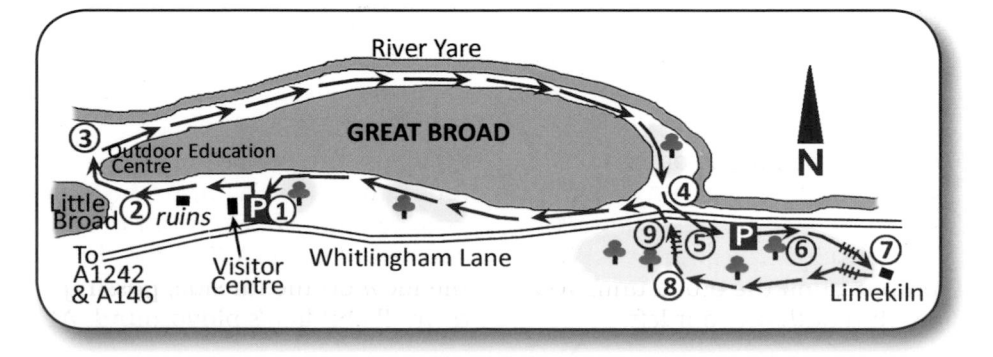

Whitlingham Great Broad and Old Wood

◆ Fun Things to See and Do ◆

There are **storyboards** along the walk. Dial the number and hear information about the walk.

During autumn look out for **blackberries** – there are lots of delicious berries to be found along the far side of the Great Broad.

Can you imagine what it would be like **chipping flints** out of the ground in the Neolithic caves? Try picking up two stones and hitting them together to break off pieces. It is very hard work, and would have taken a long time just to make one arrowhead. Take care when attempting this, as chips can fly up and hurt you.

Feed the **ducks and swans** on the southern side of the Broad. They are always hungry!

3 Go past the Outdoor Education Centre, and you will reach the meeting point of three rivers: the Yare, Tas and Wensum. Follow the path to the right. This path is slightly rougher than the one on the other side of the broad but is still suitable for pushchairs. Follow the path along the edge of the lake. This is quite a long stretch of pathway and goes past a wildfowl and wading birds conservation area. At the far end of the lake, there is a raised path to the left that can be used if the lakeside path is flooded. Continue on the path around the broad until you reach a path on your left.

4 Here you can choose *either* to follow the main path along the side of the broad back to the car park *or* to take a diversion into the woods. The woodland walk is not suitable for pushchairs as it involves some very steep gradients. *If taking the path to the Old Wood*, turn left and follow the track straight ahead, keeping the road on your right.

5 Cross the road where the footpath ends and follow the bark path to your left. Go through a car park, and walk through the meadow on the far side, passing a small children's playground. At

Kiddiwalks in Norfolk

the end of the meadow, you will see a path leading into the woods.

6 Where the path diverges, you can take the steep path upwards through the woodland, or turn left, then right and go down to see the limekiln, now home to bats.

7 At the limekiln clearing, turn right and walk up the steep flight of steps. At the top, turn left onto the bark path. This path leads across the top of the woodland, past lots of deep quarries excavated by Neolithic people. The busy A47 can be heard – but not seen – on the left-hand side. All the steep quarry sides are now covered with trees and shrubs – but there are plenty of viewpoints showing just how deep these quarries actually are.

8 The path eventually winds to the right, reaching a flight of steps leading downwards. These steps go down to the bark path beside the road. They are very, very steep and are not suitable for young children. Even older children find it a bit of a scramble. Alternatively, take the wider path to the left, which has a more gentle gradient and ends up in the car park near to the lime kilns.

9 At the bark pathway, you can choose *either* to cross the road and rejoin the walkway along the broad *or* follow the bark path to the left, through the woods and meadows back to the Great Broad car park.

◆ Background Notes ◆

The **Whitlingham Country Park** site was originally marshland. In the 1990s it was decided to extract the gravel from the area, with the ultimate intention of turning the resultant pits into new broads and nature reserves. The quarry opened in 1990 and lasted until 2008. It was restored to create the country park, which is managed by the Whitlingham Charitable Trust. The first phase comprised the Whitlingham Little Broad, a 4-hectare lake. This was followed by the Great Broad, which incorporates a rowing course, plus facilities for windsurfing, canoeing and sailing, together with a wildlife conservation area. The third and final broad –Thorpe Broad – is on the north side of the Yare and focuses on nature conservation.

17

North Burlingham

Art in the Woods

Sculpture in the woods

The Burlingham Woods are a collection of woodland areas linked by grassy tracks and fields, which hide lots of surprises. Can you find the artwork hidden in the woods? Look carefully because it changes from year to year – and can be hidden up trees or in open view within clearings. Colourful, bright and thought-provoking, it captures the attention as you walk. Bring some paper and a wax crayon and take some rubbings from the sculptured plaques en route. No two areas within this walk are the same. From ancient woodland to orchards or conifer areas, these woods offer something for everyone. It is a very relaxing walk and great fun, with something new round every corner.

Getting there North Burlingham is 8 miles east of Norwich. Burlingham Woods are just off the A47 Norwich/Great Yarmouth road. If approaching from the east turn right off the A47 to North Burlingham. It is recommended, however, to approach Burlingham from the Norwich direction as it can be difficult getting across the road; in which case turn left towards North Burlingham. You will see a turning to the left almost immediately. This leads up to the church car park.

Length of walk 2 miles.
Time 1½ hours.
Terrain Woodland paths and grassy tracks. The route is suitable for pushchairs only to point 5.
Start/Parking The free car park outside St Andrew's church (GR TG 364101).
Map OS Explorer OL40 The Broads.
Refreshments None on the route so pack a picnic to enjoy in the woods.

The Walk

1 Enter the woods by the gate at the top of the car park. Take the path to your left. This is a broad

Woodland crafts immortalised in metal for rubbing

woodland path ideal for pushchairs. Look for the sculptural plaques mounted on posts. The first one is on your left-hand side and shows the St Andrew angel.

2 Ignore the turning to the left and keep walking straight ahead.

3 Where the path diverges, with two trees in line down the centre of the path, take the left-hand turning.

4 At the end of the path, you will pass a farm building on your left-hand side before reaching a farm track. Cross the farm track and follow the sign marked 'Millennium Wood'. Take the path straight ahead through the apple trees.

5 Look for a signpost marked 'Long Plantation/Millennium Wood'. Turn left and walk up the wide pathway towards the Long Plantation. The path leads between fields on either side and is usable by pushchairs.

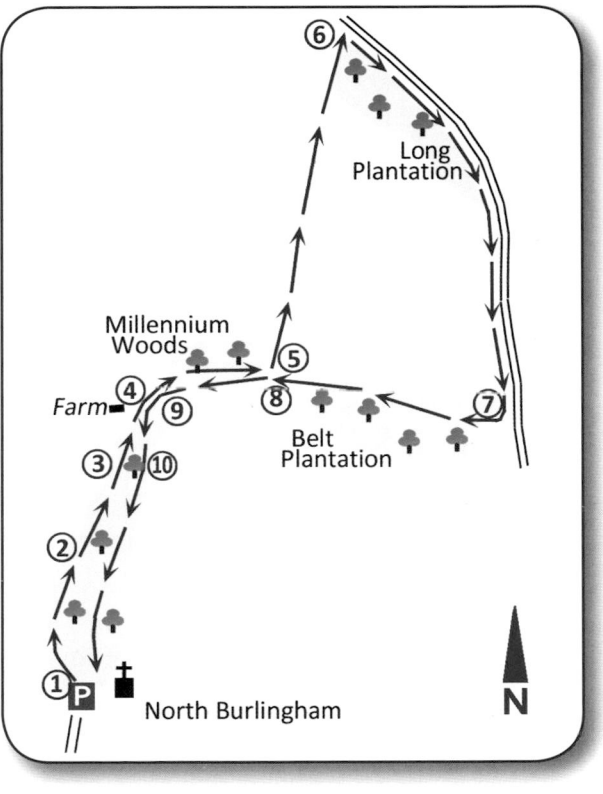

6 Turn right just before the farm gates leading onto the road. Follow the woodland track to the right. This becomes quite a narrow and rough track in places, heading through open deciduous woodland with lots of wild flowers such as campion, meadowsweet and bluebells. At the end of the path, you will reach the edge of a field. Turn left and keep walking straight ahead. This level path leads alongside the road but is separated from it by a ditch, banks and hedges. The grassy track is quite wide, and a little below the road level.

7 At the far end of the field, you will reach the Belt Plantation. The path now curves to the right. At the white marker post, turn right and walk on through the woodland. Look for a tiny plank bridge crossing a ditch on the right-hand side. Soon afterwards, you will see a willow-edged pond on your left-hand side. Listen out too for woodpeckers in this area. The path now leads slightly uphill.

8 When you come to the next signpost, take the first left and then turn left again into the Millennium Wood. This is a firm gravel/concrete surface. Look for the seat and nearby swap box. Magazines and books can be left here for swapping. If you take a book or magazine, always leave something in its place.

◆ Fun Things to See and Do ◆

Explore the sculpture trail. You can take rubbings from the plaques to make pictures of your own. All you need is a wax crayon or charcoal and some plain paper. Put the paper over the plaque and then rub hard over the surface with the crayon. This will transfer the image onto the paper. Younger children may need a little bit of help as it takes a fair amount of pressure to create a good impression.

Can you spot where **new hedging** has been created in the Millennium Wood? Tree trunks are bent over to create natural barriers. This is the traditional method of hedging. Branches grow out of the bent over trunks, and are eventually bent over again in due course.

Coppicing can be seen in the woodland, opening up the bottom storey of the woodland to encourage the growth of wild flowers.

Try moving some of the leaves on the forest floor and see what **insects** may be living underneath. Always remember to replace the leaves afterwards.

9 At the end of the path, turn to your left and cross over the road into the woodland. Follow the track straight ahead.

10 Where the track diverges around the two trees, take the left-hand turn. This path leads past the edge of the woodland, with fields on your left-hand side. Keep walking straight ahead until you reach the car park.

◆ Background Notes ◆

Burlingham Woods are used for sculpture trails and artwork inspired by natural forms. Most of these artworks are created by GCSE art students attending Acle High School. There are also numerous wooden posts upon which there are special plaques created by artist John Behm. These plaques depict local scenes and events, or things connected with the woodland – such as an Iceni horse, an angel, woad working, a lunar crescent and stars, a clouded yellow butterfly, an oak tree, bluebells, Cernunnos, a wolf, a Roman helmet, the open-field system, kingfishers. The image of Cernunnos was chosen because he was the horned god of the forest, worshipped by the Iceni who lived in this area. An unusual scene is that of the tree sitters. This tells the story of a revolt that took place 200 years ago. Local tenants and farm workers were protesting, demanding better conditions. The estate owner sought help from his neighbours to repel them, with workers using guns. Ancient bullets are still found in the area nearby.

The woods are a mix of **ancient and newly-planted woodlands**, interspersed with farmland. Depending on the season, it is possible to see bluebells, primroses, violets, wild roses, hawthorn and apple blossom, as well as fruit and berries in the autumn. Skylarks can be seen singing high above the fields in summer, while tawny and little owls live nearby. Hares, foxes and deer are frequent visitors to the woodlands, together with smaller mammals such as woodmice. Trees include oak, chestnut, ash, hawthorn, hazel, field maple, crab apple, birch and small leaved lime. The Millennium Wood was planted as an amenity woodland for local people to celebrate the millennium. Long Plantation was first created in the early 19th century, and replanted between 1945 and 1950.

18

St Benet's

Abbey Remains and Ghostly Legends

The ruined abbey at the start of the walk

This watery landscape with its flat horizons that seem to stretch for miles creates a typical Broads scene. Wrap up well no matter what the time of year, as it is very exposed and can get very windy here. Boats cruise past quietly, with the sails of yachts seemingly suspended high above the land. Artists have painted these scenes numerous times, and they never lose that special magic. Yet this walk is not just about nature – there is also an incredible mix of history, ghosts and legends!

Getting there St Benet's is about 2 miles west of the village of Ludham. Coming from the Potter Heigham direction and heading towards Wroxham on the A1062, leave Ludham and take the third turning on your left (Hall Road) as you enter Johnson Street. Take the next right and follow the road to the end. This will bring you to the parking area at St Benet's Abbey.

Length of walk 2 miles.
Time Allow at least 1½ hours.
Terrain High stiles, dirt/grass track beside river, marsh and field paths, which can be muddy after rain. Unsuitable for pushchairs. Insect repellent is recommended during late spring/summer as biting insects are common.
Start/Parking St Benet's Abbey free car park (GR TG 381158).
Map OS Explorer OL40 The Broads.
Refreshments None on the route so pack a picnic to enjoy near the river.

The Walk

1 The walk starts with a short flight of steps leading into the remains of St Benet's Abbey. Walk through the archway created between the tower and the wall.

◆ Fun Things to See and Do ◆

Look for the **signatures and dates inside the former windmill tower**. What is the earliest you can find? But do not be tempted to add your own!

Can you find the **animal carvings** high in the roof?

Look over the river and see if you can spot **Ranworth church tower**. It is often known as the Cathedral of the Broads because it is so large and tall.

Kiddiwalks in Norfolk

Don't miss going inside the remains of the mill built within the walls of the abbey gatehouse – look up and see the sky through the top of the tower. When you have finished exploring the gatehouse, head for the stile straight ahead.

2 Having crossed the stile, walk down the path to the river. Turn left and follow the path along the riverbank. Look out for yachts on the river – it is quite an amazing sight as they seem to sail through fields. As you pass the old tree near the river, look down and see a small hand-made memorial among the tree roots, filled with flowers. It is said to be a memorial to someone who died in the river but no one knows who.

3 At the end of the field, turn left and go over the stile leading into South Walsham Marshes.

4 Turn right up the slope and head for the grassy bank, which runs between two river tributaries. This route eventually joins up with the main river.

5 When the river starts to curve and you can see a building on the right-hand bank, turn and go down the bank to the lower path.

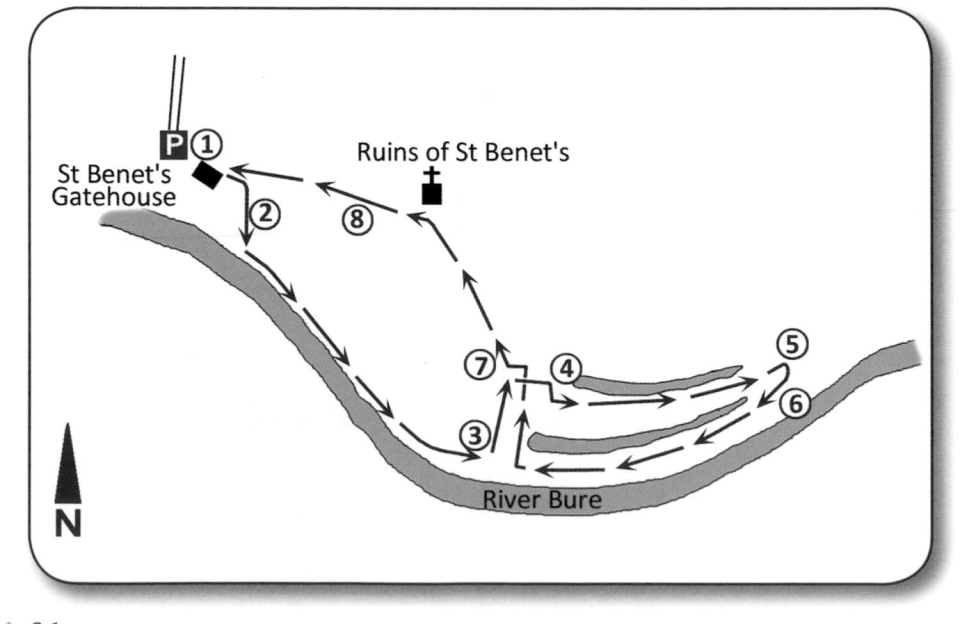

6 Walk back along the path. This runs almost parallel to the river, but follows the line of the specially created flood defences with vegetation providing a habitat for water voles and spawning fish. On a windy day, this lower path can provide some much needed shelter as the river path is very exposed.

7 Go over the stile and walk straight ahead, aiming for the cross at the top of the slope. This will lead you to the ruins of the abbey church.

8 Return to the car park by walking diagonally across the field towards the gatehouse tower and entrance stile.

◆ Background Notes ◆

St Benet's Abbey is definitely unusual and worth a visit. There was a settlement on the site by the late 10th century when it was known as St Benet-at-Holm and had become a Benedictine monastery. During the medieval period, it was responsible for 28 dependent churches and controlled a complex series of fishponds and peat diggings. By the 1500s, the monastery was declining and fell into the care of the Bishop of Norwich. To this day, the Bishop of Norwich is also known as the Abbot of St Benet's. Every year, the Bishop sails up to St Benet's and conducts a religious service on the site of the former monastic church.

The site is also home to **ghostly legends**. Brother Pacificus has been seen quietly rowing across the river in a small boat accompanied by a dog. A more dramatic legend dates from the time of the Norman Conquest. It is said that William the Conqueror struggled to take control of the abbey, and only succeeded when he bribed a monk to open the gate, by promising to make him abbot. William kept his promise – the monk immediately became the abbot of the monastery, but for only a matter of hours. That night, the new abbot was punished for his treachery by being hung from the gatehouse. It is said that late at night on 25th May, the screams of the monk can still be heard.

19

Hickling Broad

Along the Boardwalk

The boardwalk vista

Dreamy landscapes where the sky and water meet are characteristic of Hickling Broad. It is the largest expanse of open water within the Norfolk Broads area. Listen to the wind in the reeds as you walk, it is a constant sound in the background whenever you are there. Highland cows and ponies roam freely. This is a beautiful, stunning landscape, which can be very cold, desolate and exposed in wintertime. The walks are open all year, although the visitor centre is closed from October to Easter. The site is popular with bird watchers all year round – there is always something new to see. Bring a pair of binoculars and scan the sky and water for wildfowl, wading birds and much more.

Getting there Hickling Broad is off the A149 as it runs north-west from the Potter Heigham road. It is signed eastwards from Hickling village along Stubb Road.

Length of walk 1 mile of boardwalk; this can be extended for another ¾ mile along a trackway to the river.

Time About 30 minutes for the boardwalk; 1 hour for the full walk. But bear in mind that part of the full route (south of the Cadbury Hide – see point 5 on the map) is closed during the April/June breeding season.

Terrain The boardwalk is ideal for pushchairs. The extension down to the river is on a rough track. It can all get very wet in winter – even the boardwalk may be covered by thin layers of water.

Insect repellent is recommended, during late spring/summer as biting insects are common. Please note that dogs are not allowed on the Broad.

Start/Parking At the visitor centre; small charge (GR TG 428222).
Map OS Explorer OL40 The Broads
Refreshments Available at the visitor centre when open.

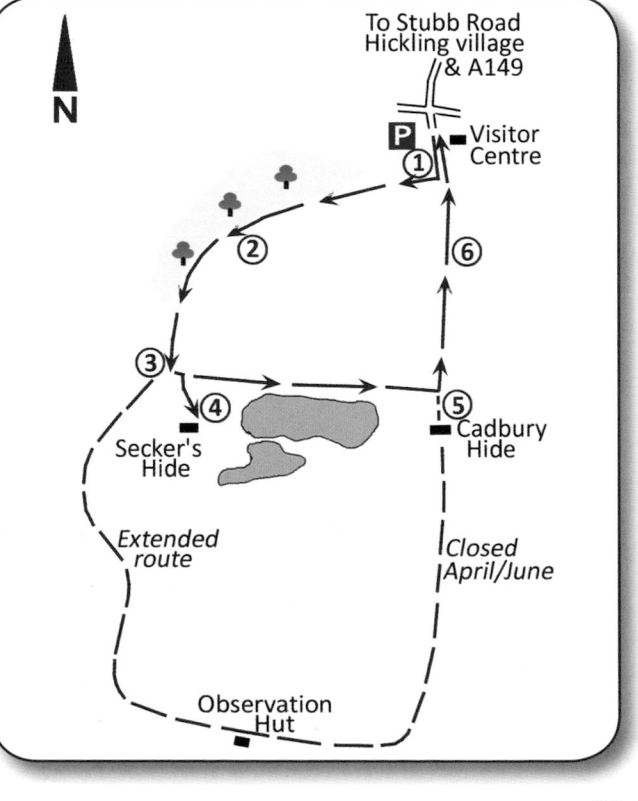

To Stubb Road
Hickling village
& A149

P — Visitor Centre
①

N

②

⑥

③

④

⑤
Cadbury Hide

Secker's Hide

Extended route

Closed April/June

Observation Hut

◆ Fun Things to See and Do ◆

There are **lots of creatures** to look for on the broads, including grazing ponies, cattle, otters, water voles, herons, dragonflies, marsh harriers, yellow and black swallowtail butterflies. **Flowers** to be found along the path include yellow flag iris, cotton grass and milk parsley.

Bring along a plastic container and try **dipping for water creatures** on the dipping platform. Always remember to carefully return them to the water afterwards.

Look for some sticks and try to **beat drum sounds** on the wooden boardwalk or fence posts just like the drummer boy would have played all those years ago.

The Walk

1 Start at the gate beside the visitor centre. Go straight ahead on the hard compacted path and through the next gate into the woodland area.

2 Follow the boardwalk path straight ahead through woodland and reed beds. This part of the boardwalk can get covered in water during winter and early spring.

3 At the path junction you have a choice. *Either* turn left and continue the boardwalk back to the centre *or* walk straight ahead down to the Observation Hut. A compacted path goes past the hut. Then take the next left turn onto a grassy track across the grazing marsh. This is a straight track to the Cadbury Hide and back onto the boardwalk.

4 *If you turn left and continue the boardwalk path,* take the next right-hand path for a visit to Secker's Hide, where you may be lucky enough to see rare bitterns and other waterfowl. Return to the boardwalk and continue to the right. The path winds past some pretty pools usually inhabited by lots of birds.

5 Look for the turning to the right – this will lead into the

Cadbury Hide, which overlooks an artificial pool known as a scrape and often attracts lots of wading birds such as redshank and snipe. Leaving the Cadbury Hide, return to the boardwalk and walk on, carefully closing the two grazing gates, which keep the cattle and horses on the marsh.

6 The boardwalk continues past a dipping platform where it is fun to dip and see what you can find – beetles, flies, tadpoles are just a few of the water creatures that may be identified. Continue down the boardwalk, passing through the gate into the car park.

◆ Background Notes ◆

Hickling Broad is one of numerous broads created in north-east Norfolk. They may look natural, but they are actually man-made. For centuries, local people dug peat from the earth as fuel for fires. As water levels rose in the late medieval times, so the peat diggings flooded and the whole environment changed to become the watery scenes we know today. Apart from the wide expanses of water, there are extensive reed beds and it is not wise to leave the paths to walk among the reeds – you can get very wet!

The atmospheric setting of Hickling Broad is ideal for **a ghost story**. If you listen carefully, you may hear the sound of a drum as a lonely drummer boy calls out to his lost love. The story goes that in the cold winter of 1813–14, John Sadler, a drummer boy in the Grenadier Guards, had returned home on leave. He fell in love with Lilly Ducker. Her father was not happy about the match and said they could meet at the riverbank – one on either side of the river. In the deep cold, the water froze and skating was possible. One night as Lilly waited at Swan Coots, she heard the swish of blades and a drum beating. John Sadler had skated across. He said that he had decided to leave the army so that they could marry. The next night, Lilly waited and waited. She heard the drum beating and skates swishing – then a crack and a splash. John Sadler had fallen into the water and was never seen again but people soon reported seeing a uniformed drummer boy skating over the water, playing his drum and whistling for Lilly.

Winterton Dunes

Down at the Seaside

The unique sand dunes at Winterton

Explore these dunes before they disappear. No one knows how long they will survive, given the strength of the North Sea. Only a few years ago, a large portion of the dunes fell into the sea during winter storms. Yet what makes them extra special is that they are totally unlike any other dunes along the Norfolk coast. The sand found here

Winterton Dunes

Getting there Winterton-on-Sea is on the north-east coast of Norfolk. It is 8 miles north of Great Yarmouth, 19 miles east of Norwich. From the A149 north of Great Yarmouth, take the B1159 through Hemsby to Winterton-on-Sea. Drive straight through the village, past the post office until you can go no further. The car park will be on your left-hand side.

Length of walk 1 mile.
Time 1¼ hours.
Terrain Sandy paths, varying gradients; not suitable for pushchairs.
Start/Parking The beach car park; small charge payable (GR TG 498198).
Map OS Explorer OL40 The Broads.
Refreshments The beach café (open every day in summer and at weekends in winter) or there is the Fisherman's Return in the village that has outdoor seating. ☎ 01493 393305.

The Walk

❶ Walk to the far end of the car park, aiming for the fishermen's huts. Turn left and walk down the wide sandy path until you see a notice-board with a map of the area on your right-hand side.

❷ Just before the notice-board there is a turning to your right. Follow the path straight ahead, keeping the gorse bushes and heather on your left and trees on your right. This is a very sandy, yet quite firm path.

❸ At the end of the small birch woodland, look for a fork in the path ahead. Just before the fork, turn sharp right onto a narrow

reflects the Baltic and is acidic. Dunes are usually ignored when visiting the beach – yet they offer a fascinating environment. Walking through them, it is possible to see just how the landscape changes – from sandy beach, through dunes being gradually colonised by grass, to the development of birch scrub and woodland. This route leads through all these different phases. Although only a short circuit, it uses up quite a lot of energy! Children can never resist running up and down the sandy dunes. Take windproof clothing as the site is very exposed and most days there is a strong breeze blowing in from the sea. If they still have some energy afterwards, the beach offers lots of possibilities for play and relaxation.

path heading for a small grove of trees. In the distance you will see a tall pole.

4 Follow the path straight ahead, aiming always for the tall pole. Look for the remains of standing fence posts on the left-hand side and views of the church tower on your right. Children will enjoy taking advantage of small side paths to run

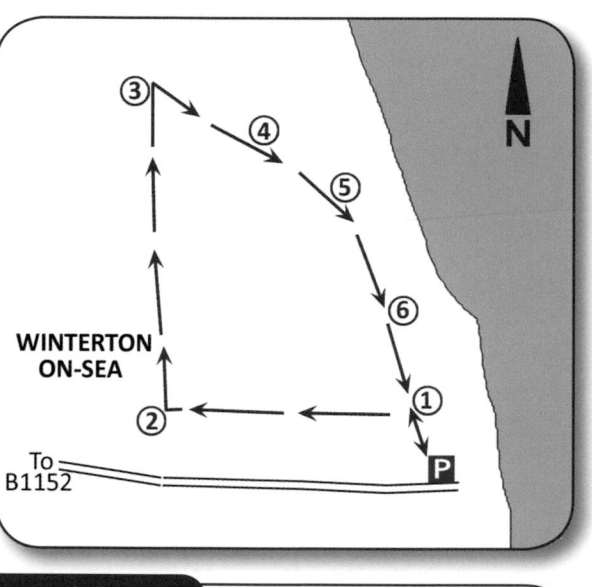

◆ Fun Things to See and Do ◆

Look out for **metal objects** of any kind – from fence posts to bases for anti-aircraft guns. These have been left over from the Second World War when the beach and dunes were heavily fortified. Do not touch anything but try and work out for what they might have been used.

Follow little paths and **run up and down the dunes**. It is quite fun, trying to run in the sand and can lead to unexpected discoveries (such as relics from the war).

Adders may be seen basking on the sand. They are perfectly safe so long as you do not try to touch them – just admire them from a distance.

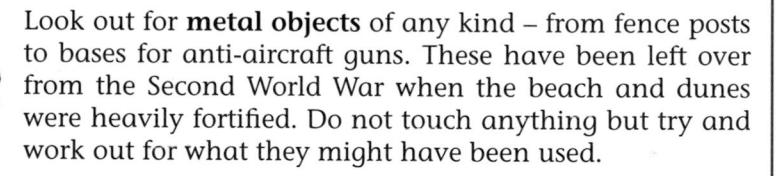

Keep an eye on the sea just over the dunes – you may see some **seals** swimming by. There is a colony of 30 to 40 seals that live just north of Winterton-on-Sea.

A touch of Africa in Norfolk

up and down the dunes. Watch where you walk – there are many lichens on the ground, several of which are quite rare.

5 When you reach the pole, you will see a track heading towards the beach café and car park. Follow this slightly winding track, which goes up and down various dunes. As you walk you will see the tower of the Coastguard watch and, on the right, the village. An unusual sight is the thatched round houses on the far edge of the dunes. These colourful creations in yellow, pink and blue form part of a holiday village.

6 When you reach a main track, turn left and walk uphill towards the fishermen's huts at the edge of the car park.

◆ Background Notes ◆

Winterton Dunes have little in common with the dunes found elsewhere on the Norfolk coast. In fact, the sand found here is similar to the acidic dune systems of the Baltic. The area shows a coastal succession of foreshore, dunes and birch scrub. It is home to a wide variety of lichens, mosses and dune grass, as well as wildlife such as natterjack toads and adders. The dunes were the first site in Britain where the southern emerald damselfly was seen. Marsh harriers hunt the area. Little terns breed here, as do stonechats, nightjars and ringed plovers. More than 170 types of bird have been recorded here during the winter as it attracts many over-wintering species.

The dunes have a **history of military use**. During the Second World War the east coast was heavily fortified against possible invasion by the Nazis. The long flat stretches of sand were regarded as a prime target for invading soldiers. Large numbers of troops were stationed at Winterton, with lots of anti-aircraft and field guns. The whole area was covered with rolls of barbed wire and pill boxes, together with landmines on the beach. There were also extensive scaffolding barriers and large numbers of anti-tank cubes. It was declared out of bounds to all local people. After the end of the war, it took many years for the area to be cleared and items are still occasionally found.

The biggest problem facing Winterton Dunes is **coastal erosion** and **rising sea levels**. Such dangers are nothing new to the area. During the 18th century, marram grass was planted to stabilise the coastline and the development of a network of dunes encouraged. Flooding and damage still occurs. In 2005 a landslide occurred during which many of the Second World War anti-tank blocks situated around the car park fell onto the beach.

An unusual feature of the area is the **Hermanus holiday camp** with its circular, thatched round houses. These are very colourful buildings visible from the car park and across the dunes. It is said that the construction of the round houses were inspired by an earlier owner of the camp who visited Hermanus Bay in South Africa.